# Planes, Trains and
# Toilet Doors

# Planes, Trains and Toilet Doors

## 50 Places That Changed British Politics

## Matt Chorley

Illustrations by Morten Mørland

WILLIAM
COLLINS

William Collins
An imprint of HarperCollins*Publishers*
1 London Bridge Street
London SE1 9GF

WilliamCollinsBooks.com

HarperCollins*Publishers*
Macken House,
39/40 Mayor Street Upper,
Dublin 1, D01 C9W8, Ireland

First published in Great Britain in 2023 by William Collins

1

ISBN 978-0-00-862206-0 (Hardback)

Set in Garamond MT Std

Printed and bound in Bosnia and Herzegovina by GPS Group.

This book is produced from independently certified FSC™ paper
to ensure responsible forest management.

For more information visit: www.harpercollins.co.uk/green

*For Alyson, Emily and Jessica*

# Contents

## Homes

## Travel

# Introduction

March 2010. Aged 27, I am standing in the back of a mint-green VW campervan called Maisy, sniffing a pint of milk to see if it is off. Sitting with his legs hanging out of the door of the van, my guest is complaining that my Hobnobs are soft. Within a few weeks he will be deputy prime minister, except neither of us knows it yet.

We are in Cornwall. I am midway through my Marginal Mystery Tour of the swing seats spread across my patch as London editor of the *Western Morning News*, an important newspaper in Devon, Cornwall and Somerset back then of course because they didn't have the internet. Or television. Or electricity. As a child of the Somerset Levels I am allowed to make these jokes. I'd been in two minds about even bothering with the detour to meet Nick Clegg, the youthful leader of the Liberal Democrats with a mere walk-on part in the blockbuster battle between Gordon Brown and David Cameron, but the sun was out and it would make some easy copy.

I had swung Maisy off the road onto the gravel car park of a Cornish tin-mining company, and a Lib Dem press officer came bowling over very enthusiastically. They are always enthusiastic, Lib Dem press officers. They're just glad to see anybody, to be honest. So he pops his head through the window of the van and says: 'Great. Have you got the refreshments?' What? 'I've got down here on my itinerary here, it says "Matt Chorley is provid-ing refreshments".' He was right. That is what it said. But he was also wrong. They had got the wrong idea about the campervan. I hadn't been sleeping in it, because it was so cold and wet and miserable in March, instead opting for pubs, B&Bs and mates'

sofas. So I also hadn't kept tabs on the four-pint bottle of milk
I'd bought a week earlier. And that's how I ended up in the back
of a campervan detecting the dairy to make sure I didn't poison
the man who would soon, amazingly, be the second most powerful politician in the country. I could have changed the course
of political history with a curdled coffee. Given how the next
five years were to unfold for the Lib Dems, Clegg probably
wishes I had.

The direction of British politics, and with it my life, your
life and those of other less important people, has been decided
on less, and in even more extraordinary and ordinary places.
So much – arguably too much – of our daily national political
conversation is about Number 10, Whitehall and the Houses
of Parliament; the shenanigans of the weird inhabitants of the
so-called Westminster village – a village no normal person
would want to move to – as they strut the corridors of power,
whispering in corners, practising high politics and low skulduggery, and feeling terribly important. And yet so many of the key
turning points, which have decided who runs the country (and
doesn't) and how they run it (or don't), have taken place not in
the mock-Gothic, crumbling corridors and courtyards of the
Palace of Westminster or the higgledy-piggledy terraced houses
of Downing Street, nor in the windowless, halitosis hotspots of
party conferences. Instead they have played out in towns and
cities and villages across the country. Unlikely, often humdrum
places, where accidents happen that change everything.

I have spent two decades reporting from Westminster, joining
the press gallery when Tony Blair was prime minister, and David
Cameron was on course to lose to David Davis in the Tory leadership contest. Since then I've interviewed six of the last seven
people who made it to be prime minister, and reported from
Downing Street and Brussels, from the Houses of Parliament,
Holyrood. In theory these are the places where the big moments
happen. Yet history is not fussy, and can be made, in fact prefers
to be made, away from the gaze of people like me. It unfolds at

politicians' kitchen tables, in downstairs loos and in the beds they weren't meant to be sleeping in. The everyday happens every day. There is a brilliant scene in Armando Iannucci's satire *In The Loop*, a big-screen spin-off of *The Thick of It*, where Simon Foster, a British government minister played by Tom Hollander, has to break away from attempts to prevent an Anglo-US invasion of a Middle Eastern country to deal with an eccentric constituent complaining about an unstable wall. Global politics must play second fiddle to the local. This portrayal of the constituency link retained by MPs and ministers alike sums up why British politics remains fascinating, and reassuringly unpredictable. It is why prime ministers on parade get buttonholed by members of the public wherever they are, even if the TV cameras are watching. Perhaps especially if the TV cameras are watching.

This book celebrates those stories. The town halls and train stations; car parks and coffee shops; dentists' chairs and desolate hillsides; beach huts and boarding schools where politicians changed history – most of the time without meaning to. So I drew up a few self-imposed rules: none of the places which changed politics could be in Westminster. They all had to be events that can at least tangentially be said to have changed politics. Sometimes the impact was instant – a new prime minister taking power – other times it would take months, even years, for the impact of the event to be felt, a political butterfly effect. And I wanted them to be unknown stories, not just well-worn tales told many times before. All of these rules are broken in the pages that follow.

While I have sought a geographical and historical spread, the list is inevitably biased to the events and places I have witnessed, or picked up along the way. The events are spread unevenly over the past 250 years, and across the UK. The whole project has been quite the journey, across the country and through time. It's taken me from a tiny museum in the pretty fishing village of Lossiemouth to an even smaller convenience store in central London, and I've gone deep into the National Archives at Kew, and the National Theatre Archive at Waterloo, and deeper still into one particular swimming pool. I have visited many of the places, though not all. In fact, at most there isn't really anything to look at. No so much as a blue plaque. Quite right too. No one likes a fuss. It would be horribly un-British.

Before beginning this project I'd assumed that the lesson, if there were any, to learn from it would be that politics can happen in the most unlikely of places. Which is true. But more than that this collection serves as a reminder that the word 'unprecedented' should be used sparingly in politics, perhaps not at all. Almost everything which consumes the breathless Twitter commentariat who claim never to have seen the like of it has happened before, and better (or worse, depending on your point of view). Dramatic campaign speeches, futuristic technology, eye-catching stunts, surprise election results, quick changes of government, shock resignations, untimely deaths, chance meetings, sex scandals, money scandals, legal scandals, have all been done before. Whoever is the next minister caught saying or doing something unprecedented, remember the speed cameras and the sand dunes and the toothpaste in the dark. Whenever the next unprecedented reshuffle happens, remember that at least nobody died in the middle of it. Whichever unprecedented scenes unfold during a by-election, watch to see if anybody leaves the polling station via a window. Whatever the next unprecedented war of words, be glad that it does not end in actual pistols at dawn.

What follows is also not intended to be *the* fifty places which changed politics – there are obviously far more than that – it is merely *a* collection of fifty places. It is, like all politics, inevitably subjective. I have no doubt that you will think of better ones that I have not included. I have no doubt that you will disagree with some I have chosen. Many of those involved will no doubt argue about their significance, from the aspiring party leader locked in the bathroom to the owners of the first prime ministerial legs to be seen on display. I hope at least some will be your cup of tea. Sorry about the milk.

*Schools and hospitals*

# 1

# Dr Addington's surgery, 7 Clifford Street, London

*Christmas 1773*

William Pitt was very, very clever, but very, very ill. Aged just 14, he went to study at Cambridge in October 1773, but within a few weeks he was taken ill and spent two months confined to his rooms before travelling back to Hayes, the family home in Bromley, Kent. It was here that he was referred to Dr Anthony Addington, who had for many years from smart offices in Piccadilly served as physician to his father, William Pitt the Elder, who had been prime minister in the 1760s. A fellow of the Royal College of Physicians, Addington practised in the treatment of insanity and was among the medics called to treat the madness of King George III.

However, his recommendation for young Pitt's appalling gout was to have far-reaching consequences. It included extra sleep and fewer late nights studying, along with a better diet – all perfectly sensible – alongside the more eccentric if harmless requirement of regular exercise on horseback. More extreme, and consequential, was the prescription of port. Daily. Yes, daily doses of port to deal with gout. The exact quantity of port wine is lost to history, but it was a lot, maybe a bottle a day, maybe more, 'but at any rate a good deal of it' according to Pitt's biographer

William Hague (who knows a thing or two about this area, having once claimed he spent his youth drinking fourteen pints of beer a day).

The prescription was strict advice that Pitt characteristically followed to the letter, and remarkably his health improved. He returned to Cambridge, where he became friends with future slavery campaigner William Wilberforce, before training as a lawyer and being called to the Bar in 1780 and entering the Commons a year later, where he quickly demonstrated the power of his oratory and argument. He was chancellor by the age of just 24, and a year later in December 1783 he followed in his father's footsteps in becoming prime minister – the youngest ever, before or since. Initially his government was mocked as the 'mince pie administration' because it was thought it would not last until Christmas. Instead he battled on, surviving Commons defeats, winning over the public and then securing a victory in an election, and he remained in office for a total of almost eighteen years.

And still he kept drinking the port. In fact in later life he became known as a 'three-bottle man', which sounds like a lot by today's standards, but port in the late eighteenth century was weaker than it is today and the bottles were smaller. Even so, it was still equivalent to more than a bottle and a half of today's booze, and his reliance on alcohol showed in tales of him having the shakes, and downing tumblers of the stuff before his infamous, barnstorming Commons speeches. He was not alone. In fact, Pitt's entire cabinet had a reputation for being almost constantly plastered. Having survived the ill-health and duels of his first spell as PM, his second from 1804 to 1806 was dominated by the Napoleonic Wars and marked by a number of defeats to the French, including the Battle of Austerlitz in December 1805. Indeed, some suggested that this loss may have finally broken Pitt's health. In truth, he was not a well man and had not been for some time. The Duke of Wellington would later argue that Pitt's health had been 'destroyed by long and previous exertions in the House of Commons, and by deluging his stomach with port wine and water, which he drank to excess, in order to give a false and artificial stimulus to his nervous system'.

On 16 January 1806 Pitt took to his sickbed, and he died on 23 January at the age of just 46. Life expectancy was not much higher for the average man in those days, but Pitt was far from average and could have enjoyed many more years at the top of politics. He never saw his friend Wilberforce fulfil their hope of abolishing slavery. Even so, he was prime minister for almost nineteen of the last twenty-three years of his life. In fact, during the period when he was out of office he was replaced by his friend Henry Addington, the son of the doctor who had prescribed him port all those years earlier.

# 2

# Gillygate School, Pontefract

*Thursday, 15 August 1872*

It is a time-honoured tradition that for many children an election means a day off school. This is not, though, born of an attempt to engender feelings of positivity towards democracy among the nation's youth: it is mere practicality. The polling stations have to go somewhere, and often that means taking over schools.

When the first secret ballot was held in the West Yorkshire town of Pontefract, the local schools were judged large enough to address concerns that those who were on their way in to vote should not meet those who had already cast their ballot coming out. It was just one of the new rules designed to end the culture of intimidation, bribery and corruption which had grown up around Britain's early forays in direct democracy. Previously a clerk would call out the name of a voter in a packed room and they would have to shout back whom they were supporting, with full lists of how each person voted often published in newspapers and books.

All that changed with the Ballot Act 1872, which had become law in July that year, and in August a by-election was held in Pontefract under the (since abandoned) convention that if the local MP was appointed a minister, their constituency should have a say on whether they should remain in the Commons. Hugh Childers, the incumbent Liberal MP for Pontefract, had been named chancellor of the Duchy of Lancaster and paymaster general by Gladstone, so had to defend his seat against the Conservative John Savile.

Under the new secret ballot rules each polling booth had a presiding officer sitting at a table, joined by an assistant, a clerk and a 'personating agent' for each candidate, apparently to stop voters claiming to be someone who they were not. At 8 a.m. the presiding officer tipped his ballot box over to show it was empty, then locked it with a key and sealed it with wax. This being Pontefract, the wax was sealed with the stamp used to make cakes at the local Dunhills liquorice factory. And so the voting could begin.

What is striking about accounts of that first vote is how similar it is to casting ballots today: voters came in, received a ballot paper and were shown to one of four compartments erected in the room, where they found a pencil with which to make their mark, then folded up the paper and posted it into the ballot box.

Not everything went smoothly. In one polling station the compartments were so shoddy that when four people were in them, gaps meant one voter could see how his neighbour on each side was voting. When an illiterate voter turned up everyone had to leave, including the police officer on duty to keep the peace, so that the presiding officer could help him while preserving the secrecy of his vote.

Getting in and out of the polling station was also not straightforward. While most of the chosen venues worked just fine, at the schoolroom on Gillygate in Pontefract the layout was problematic. Voters leaving would pass those arriving. So, with amazing ingenuity, a window was knocked out and wooden boards were laid in a steep incline to the level of the windowsill so people who had voted could leave through the window and walk down the planks into the schoolyard. This was not without risk; the angle and the fact that the boards were bending did not help, as *The Times* reported the next day: 'The voter, full of grave and serious thoughts at having assisted at so important an experiment, found himself involuntarily running with an ever-increasing impetus down a steep incline on a spring board which would have enabled a professional gymnast to clear the school wall with the greatest ease. A few envious observers beguiled the tedious moments by watching the egress of the voters from this polling division under the impression that the Council Office had adopted some patent apparatus for carrying out the directions of the Act that the voter shall leave the polling booth with the utmost possible expedition.' Sadly, polling station springboards did not become a permanent fixture of all future elections.

Voting closed at 4 p.m., with the ballot boxes sent to Pontefract town hall. At 8 p.m. it was announced that 1,236 votes had been cast, an unremarkable turnout of just under two-thirds, and Childers had retained his seat with 53 per cent of the vote. So being a secret vote did not change the political map, but it did change the atmosphere. Locals complained that it was so quiet they would not have known there was an election on. It was almost boring. No riots, no breach of the peace, no claims of bribery. Everyone welcomed it. Well, maybe not Pontefract's publicans. The *Times* report concluded: 'Persons of great experience declare that they never saw a contested election in which less intoxicating liquor was drunk.'

# 3

# Tredegar General Hospital

*Saturday, 7 April 1928*

Who can forget Winston Churchill intoning: 'If you're going through hell, keep going.' Or Jim Callaghan asking: 'Crisis? What crisis?' Or even Sarah Palin boasting: 'I can see Russia from my house.' Like all the best political quotations, they never actually said it. And to that list we might add Aneurin Bevan, the stuttering son of a coal miner who would go on to create the National Health Service, famously declaring that it was inspired by his home town: 'All I am doing is extending to the entire population of Britain the benefits we had in Tredegar for a generation or more. We are going to "Tredegar-ise" you.'

Except he did not say it. Or at least nobody can find evidence of it. Nick Thomas-Symonds, the Labour MP and Bevan biographer, tells me: 'Neither Michael Foot [another Bevan biographer] nor me could actually source it properly. It's one of those things everyone thinks he said, and it sounds like he might have, but we can't pin it down. I think he may well have said it. It's a shame we can't prove it.'

Whether he said he actually stated his aim to 'Tredegar-ise' the nation or not, he did it, drawing on his experience in the Welsh valleys mining town to transform health care and housing across the UK. By the time Bevan was elected to the town's cottage hospital management committee on 7 April 1928, and became chairman a year later, the Tredegar Workmen's Medical Aid Society had been looking after its members for almost forty years. It was in essence a collective, with first miners and then later their families and other townsfolk paying twopence or thruppence in the pound each week in return for help with medical care. By the 1920s, when Bevan became involved, it had five or six doctors, two dentists, pharmacists, nurses and a hospital. Everything from drugs and X-rays to artificial limbs, spectacles and even wigs was covered. If the local medics could not help, patients would be sent further afield to Newport, Cardiff or even Bristol, Bath and London, with a first-class train ticket thrown in. By the early 1930s it covered 95 per cent of the local population. The society was not unique – community funds had sprung up all over – but when defending the NHS's formation in the Commons years later Bevan boasted: 'In my native town of Tredegar we had one of the pioneer schemes in Great Britain.'

Thomas-Symonds agrees. 'Much has been made of the Medical Aid Society as a model for the NHS, and indeed its principles of operation are very similar, save that the NHS was paid for from general taxation, not specific contributions,' he wrote in his biography, *Nye: The Political Life of Aneurin Bevan*. 'Bevan's formative experience in providing healthcare was undoubtedly the Medical Aid Society.'

Yet ironically the societies would not survive the Tredegar boy's greatest triumph: the creation of the NHS. It was born out of the Second World War, when every local hospital, large or small, and, crucially, their doctors and nurses had been brought into a single national effort. In July 1945 Bevan was appointed minister of health in the post-war Attlee government, and he proposed doing the same thing in peacetime, running health care nationally from the Ministry of Health. He declared: 'If a hospital bedpan is dropped in a hospital corridor in Tredegar, the reverberations should echo around Whitehall.'

The Conservatives voted against it repeatedly. Hospital doctors, in particular, hated it, and Bevan was forced to buy them off. 'I stuffed their mouths with gold.' GPs would get similar treatment. There were rows about who should get what, who should pay, and what staff should be paid. Those rows continue to this day, with Brits enjoying a strange relationship with an arm of the state that they love to praise and criticise in the same breath. Nigel Lawson, who was Margaret Thatcher's longest-serving chancellor, once wrote: 'The NHS is the closest thing the English have to a religion.' Indeed, it was given pride of place in the opening ceremony of the 2012 London Olympics. Imagine doing that for the Department for Work and Pensions.

Yet in the twenty-first century the NHS struggles under the twin pressures of rising costs of new, successful treatments and the happy consequence of that success being that we all live longer. Today people survive conditions that the Tredegar Workmen's Medical Aid Society could not have saved them from, but that comes with an extraordinary price tag. In 1950, the NHS cost about £460 million. Today, when adjusted for inflation, it is some ten times higher, yet the economy has only grown by five times in real terms. The need for long-term work-force planning has been overlooked in favour of short-term political advantage. The legacy for Tredegar itself is little better: while it is hailed by many as the birthplace of the NHS, parts of the town are in the top 10 per cent of the most deprived areas in Wales, including on health outcomes. Tredegar General Hospital, which so inspired Bevan when he had helped to run it, was shut down in 2010. After being boarded up for years it has since been demolished to make way for a new health and well-being centre, a step towards regeneration in a once-mighty industrial town where many buildings that were key not just to its own history, but that of the nation, have been left to crumble.

Bevan, though, was a believer in helping people, not preserving institutions or buildings for the sake of it. Henry Richard Jones, a medic and the grandfather of Welsh comedy actor and writer Ruth Jones, ran a medical aid society in Porthcawl. When the NHS was created he wrote to Bevan asking for the societies to remain involved. Bevan wrote back (and this is a real quote): 'You have shown us the way and by your very efficiency you have brought about your own cessation.'

# 4

# Shrewsbury School

*Tuesday, 30 November 1954*

In 1552 Edward VI founded a school in Shropshire, delivering on demands first made to his father, Henry VIII, to use money raised from his dissolution of ecclesiastical establishments for educational purposes. Since then it has taught the great and the good, including Old Salopians who went on to be deputy prime minister (Michael Heseltine), pioneer of the theory of evolution (Charles Darwin) and conquerer of Everest (Charles Evans).

Yet 400 years after its founding, this most Establishment of educational establishments would also bring together a quartet of pupils who would go on to make a career out of mocking the great and good, and in doing so not just change attitudes towards politicians but change the political lexicon too.

Christopher Booker and Paul Foot met on the day they went to take the Shrewsbury scholarship exam. They bonded immediately. William Rushton and Richard Ingrams had arrived together on the same day too. Booker and Ingrams both sang in the choir. Foot and Ingrams did classics together. Ingrams and Rushton were in the same house. Their paths criss-crossed, and would do for the next decade, a thread which leads to the founding of *Private Eye*, the satirical magazine in whose pages politicians (and political journalists) both fear and delight to appear.

Not that it was clear that this is where these boys were heading. 'These people were quite unnoticed when they were at Shrewsbury,' recalled their headmaster, John Peterson, in *The Private Eye Story*. Ingrams he remembered as 'a very able boy, a classical scholar, no trouble at all, a model boy'. Booker was an 'extraordinarily staid young man, reserved and studious, used to spend his Sundays collecting fossils'. Foot had 'all the makings of an angry young man, but he was not in fact a difficult boy at school'. Rushton was 'undistinguished' until he took a part in a school play, and never recovered from his experience of the limelight, but even by then 'he had one talent: he was a good cartoonist'.

On 30 November 1954 a tree was planted at Shrewsbury outside the school to mark the fourth centenary of the birth of Sir Philip Sidney, the Elizabethan poet and former pupil. But the boys were in no mood for reverence. Having been contributors to *The Salopian*, the school newspaper, Ingrams and Rushton took charge of a special edition dated 1554, apparently published by William Caxton, the printing press pioneer. It mocked school traditions and events. Laurence Le Quesne, the teacher responsible for the newspaper, later told Ingrams' biographer, Harry Thompson, that the jokes were 'slightly deflating, without being really unkind enough to be called satirical'. But they had been bitten by the bug, and would go on to carve out a reputation for their jokes about the teachers. The pages of *The Salopian* also debuted the Pseud, short for pseudo-intellectual, a creation of Ingrams' under the name Otis, which would go on to have its own Corner, and enter the dictionary and the national vocabulary. When Ingrams and Rushton's time in charge ended, Booker and Foot, a year younger, took over. The roles which emerged back then remain the pillars of the *Eye* even today. Ingrams provided the jokes. Rushton the cartoons. Foot offered a strain of seriousness. Booker pure contrarianism.

Spells in national service followed Shrewsbury, and then, for some, university. Ingrams was pleasantly surprised to find Foot at Oxford, where they got involved first in a paper called *Parson's*

*Pleasure* and later *Mesopotamia*, with Rushton popping up from London at weekends to draw cartoons. *Mesopotamia* was edited by another undergraduate, Peter Usborne, and after they suffered the indignity of their student days coming to an end, he suggested that the magazine need not. It could continue out in the real world, just as the age of deference was beginning to crumble and the sixties were starting to swing.

Names for this new publication were tricky. *The Yellow Press*, *The British Letter*, *The Flesh's Weekly*, *The Bladder* and *The Finger* were all rejected before *Private Eye* won through, largely by being the idea with the fewest objections. The first issue appeared on 25 October 1961, in the same month as Peter Cook had opened the Establishment Club as a home for live satirical comedy. The magazine had been largely pasted together on the floor of Rushton's bedroom in his mother's house, but rode the wave of the satire boom that was soon also being fuelled on TV by *That Was The Week That Was*.

After a bumpy start it found an audience, and then a buyer in Cook, which meant it had a future too. But its founders' past still hung thick in the air. Marking the *Eye*'s first decade, one of the magazine's original contributors, John Wells, wrote in *The Guardian*: 'The atmosphere of the Prefect's Study before a beating is still heavy in the office when the entire Shrewsbury gang is gathered together.'

Ian Hislop, who replaced Ingrams as editor in 1986, tells me that the *Eye* simply would not exist without Shrewsbury. 'It's an extraordinary coincidence of talent. They all essentially wanted to just question the official narrative at all points. And I'm presuming that comes from being at a certain type of school at a certain time.'

Not that this friendship forged at school meant it was all plain sailing. Despite their history – in fact, maybe because of it – there were endless fights and feuds. When Booker, the first editor of the *Eye*, went on honeymoon in 1963, Ingrams staged a coup and replaced him. It was two years before Booker returned to the magazine, where he then remained for years as part of the joke-writing team with Ingrams, Hislop and cartoonist Barry Fantoni. Foot, who became increasingly left-wing, would leave periodically to write elsewhere before always returning. 'Because they'd all been sort of forged at the same place, they were all both obsessed by each other and complemented each other for the rest of their lives,' Hislop says. 'Those friendships were incredibly strong.'

Rushton died in 1996, followed by Foot in 2004 and Booker in 2019. Yet *Private Eye*, still looking like the home-made effort glued together on Mrs Rushton's carpet, survives. Hislop's refusal to put it online has secured print sales of quarter of a million copies every fortnight, poking fun at all-comers, as it always has. The very first edition took aim at the cult around an ageing Winston Churchill, who remained a back-bench MP, teased Harold Macmillan, the old Etonian PM, and even John F. Kennedy, who at 44 was being mocked for being too old and a cartoon suggested he might make way for a younger man. Two years later, when Harold Wilson became Labour leader his carefully cultivated public image was ridiculed with a cartoon showing him returning home and removing his face to reveal a blank behind. His wife would become a regular in the spoof 'Mrs Wilson's Diary', taking the reader behind the suburban scenes of a PM. It was a trick repeated with the 'Dear Bill' letters, supposedly written by Denis Thatcher. When John Smith died in 1994, the *Eye* front cover featured a newspaper seller saying, 'He'd still beat Major.' Tony Blair was named 'Tony Bliar, 23' before he even became Labour leader. Gordon Brown was 'The Supreme Leader'. David Cameron was mocked up as lord of the manor in Downturn Abbey. Nobody was spared.

In fact, much of the way we talk about politics today originates from the pages of the *Eye*. 'Ugandan discussions' as a euphemism for sex, after a journalist allegedly had an encounter with a former Ugandan cabinet minister. 'Tired and emotional' for being drunk, after the BBC used it to describe Labour's alcoholic deputy leader George Brown. Sir Bufton Tufton as the archetypal shire Tory

MP. Dave Spart as the archetypal leftie agitator. *The Daily Tele-graph* is the *Torygraph*. The typo-prone *Guardian* is *The Grauniad*.

But to what end? That the *Eye*'s founders did not agree politi-cally explains why the magazine's politics is hard to discern in the stream of long-running jokes. 'All satirical jokes are there to make a point,' Hislop says. 'I don't think they're there to make a tribal political point.' In an age when the jokes get elected, maybe we are just beyond satire. 'People always say that,' Hislop adds. 'The first writer I know who said satire was pointless was Juvenal. He was the Roman satirist writing in AD 100. Nothing is beyond satire. You just have to work harder.' Politics in the past decade has given plenty of material, the *Eye* lasting longer than any of the people it satirises, and Hislop seeing himself as the long-serving king of satire: 'You think, Oh, there's another prime minister now. Do come in. We'll see how you do.'

# 5

# Middlesex Hospital

*Friday, 18 January 1963*

At just after 9 p.m. Dora called out from the private side room to a nearby nurse that she thought her husband was struggling. Having rested peacefully for several hours, he had made a sudden movement. The nurse summoned Dr Walter Somerville, a consultant cardiologist at the hospital. The 56-year-old's patient's heart condition had deteriorated suddenly. The doctor was at the bedside within seconds. It was too late. At 9.12 p.m. no more could be done. Dora clasped her husband's hand as he slipped away.

At 9.14 p.m. Peter Clark entered a nearby room in the hospital to break the news: 'It was suddenly and peacefully two minutes ago.' The Party press officer was informing a room of journalists so that they would tell the world that Hugh Gaitskell, Labour leader of the opposition on the verge of securing power, was dead.

Gaitskell's daughters Cressida and Julia, waiting in a ground-floor room, were called upstairs to join their mother in grief. Outside the imposing red-brick façade of the Middlesex Hospital the country began to mourn the loss of the man who would have been their prime minister. Who had faced down the left of his party. Who had seemed certain to end a decade and a half of Conservative rule.

The Queen wrote of her 'deep distress' at the news, while Harold Macmillan, the Conservative prime minister, declared his premature death 'a grievous loss to the whole nation'. Clement Attlee, the former Labour PM, said: 'Had he been spared at the next election, I believe he would have returned to power as Labour Prime Minister.' JFK sent a tribute to his political ally, with whom he had bonded over a lunch of steak tournedos anversoise and Californian rosé at the White House less than a year earlier: 'His strength of character, force of intelligence and generosity of purpose made him one of the foremost figures in the Western community.' Tributes arrived from leaders across the globe and political spectrum. Perhaps the most striking symbol of his broad public appeal is that, after he was hospitalised, at least seventeen members of the public offered to donate him their kidney.

Gaitskell had struggled with his health, exacerbated by his tendency to carry the weight of office heavily. Before Christmas 1962 he fell ill with flu and was admitted to Manor House Hospital in Golders Green, but was pictured smiling for cameras as he was discharged on 23 December to spend Christmas with his family. A workaholic, he was looking forward to a New Year trip to Russia to meet Soviet premier Nikita Khrushchev. Instead the virus flared up again, leading to pleurisy, and doctors warned him that a trip to freezing Moscow in the winter would make it worse. It got worse anyway, and on Friday, 4 January he was readmitted to hospital, this time the Middlesex Hospital, one of London's oldest medical centres a couple of blocks from Oxford Street, with a recurrence of the virus infection on his left lung. As concern grew, so too did the team working to keep him alive, swelling to nine specialist doctors over the following fortnight.

Late on the night of Thursday, 17 January Gaitskell was taken to an operating theatre to be put on a kidney dialysis machine, delivered from St Paul's Hospital by a police van. During the night a power cut in the streets nearby raised fears that his treatment would be affected, but the lights stayed on. By the following morning doctors were reporting that 'large quantities of poison had been extracted', but at 8.30 a.m. on Friday it was turned off, with medics worried it was putting added strain on his heart, which was getting weaker. It was a Catch-22 – treating one symptom was making another worse.

Gaitskell returned to his room in the private wing of the hospital, the same room where Winston Churchill had been treated for a broken leg a year earlier. Gaitskell continued to be given blood through a drip, while Dora sat by his side all day and into the evening, with no visitors aside from doctors and nurses. And then the end came. John Harris, a Labour Party spokesman, said the doctors 'had rarely seen such courage' in a patient. 'A light has gone out of our lives.'

Widely praised for retaining his scholar's integrity, Gaitskell was not a natural politician. As a junior minister he once suggested people save energy by not washing. 'Personally, I have never had a great many baths.' On another occasion he started crying while addressing a meeting of miners, choking on his tears. But he had grown in stature during his seven years as Labour leader.

The son of an official in the Indian Civil Service, he went to Winchester before reading philosophy, politics and economics at Oxford, during which time he was radicalised to the socialist cause by the treatment of workers during the 1926 general strike. He embarked on a career in academia, and later as a private secretary in Whitehall. First elected as an MP in Leeds in the post-war election of 1945, he was a minister within two years and chancellor of the exchequer by 1950, just five years after entering the Commons – a meteoric rise later matched by Rishi Sunak. He experienced life in opposition for the first time in 1951, when Churchill returned as PM. After Attlee went on to lose the 1955 election to Conservative Anthony Eden, he resigned. Gaitskell became Labour leader of the opposition, winning the support of more MPs than his opponents Aneurin Bevan and Herbert Morrison combined. Bevan had apparently taken a swipe at his dry rival, a little unfairly, as 'a desiccated calculating machine', although he later denied it was aimed at Gaitskell.

After spending four years as Labour leader, at the 1959 election Labour again lost, Macmillan pulling off a surprise win for the Conservatives – not unlike John Major's expectation-defying 1992 victory. Gaitskell conceded defeat at 1 a.m., despite many seats having not declared. He remained as leader, though, and the fight with the left continued. Believing that public opposition to nationalisation was in part to blame for the election defeat, Gaitskell launched an attempt to rewrite Clause IV of Labour's constitution, which committed to 'the common ownership of the means of production, distribution and exchange'. He was defeated by the left, and it would be thirty-six years before Tony Blair finished what Gaitskell started. However, when his party conference defied him to back unilateral disarmament he vowed to 'fight, fight and fight again to save the party we love'. He did, and it worked, surviving the power struggle stronger for it. But his body could not match his political strength.

*The Times* said his political integrity was his most precious quality: 'It fortified him to endure electoral defeat, the defection of associates, and much mis-understanding over his attempts to modernise the party's constitution.' *The Guardian* described his death as 'a personal, political, and national tragedy', adding: 'The tragedy is that a man of immense courage and integrity has been taken away just when he was most likely to be needed.' The London *Evening Standard* said: 'In greater measure than anyone now active in Parliament he had the goodwill and respect of millions who did not share his political views.' Cassandra in the *Daily Mirror* wrote: 'Everything was within his grasp – except life itself.'

Alongside the eulogies, the papers were immediately filled with speculation about who might replace him and what that might mean for Labour, which had seemed on course to oust the Conservatives after more than a decade. By the next election in 1964 both leaders were new: Harold Wilson had replaced

Gaitskell and Macmillan had resigned, leaving Alec Douglas-Home as prime minister to lead the Conservatives to defeat in October 1964. Gaitskell's victory became Wilson's. His legacy lived on: his followers, dubbed Gaitskellites, continued to carry the torch, including Anthony Crosland, James Callaghan and Roy Jenkins.

Ten years after Gaitskell's death, Jenkins wrote in *The Times*: 'He would not have been a perfect prime minister.' But he concluded that he would have won bigger than Wilson, and would have been a better prime minister to serve under. In the 1960s, politics and the country had been stunned by Gaitskell's sudden death. Before the century was out, and before Labour could secure a solid, lasting grip on power, the party and the country would experience the same shattering loss in 1994 with the death of John Smith, an agreeable, quietly determined leader on course for power.

# 6

# Eton

There are many reasons I have not become prime minister. Not going to university probably hasn't helped – just eight of the fifty-seven PMs in our history didn't have a degree. Although it's notable that they include the Duke of Wellington, Winston Churchill and Benjamin Disraeli, as well as more recent non-graduates John Major and Jim Callaghan. Going to the right school also helps: twenty of the fifty-seven went to Eton. But having the right teacher perhaps matters most. And I was never taught by Eric Anderson.

A tall, slightly stooped, kindly man, Anderson, it seems, was a political genius. Or a disaster, depending on how you think the country has been run for most of the past quarter-century. After studying English at St Andrews and Oxford, he went straight into teaching, beginning a career which would help shape modern Britain in a way he could never have predicted. He first joined Fettes College, the elite Edinburgh school, before moving to Gordonstoun, the rather grim Scottish boarding school where one of his pupils was the future King Charles. Between bouts of homesickness and bullying, the young prince was coaxed by Anderson into taking the lead role in a production of *Macbeth*.

Having bagged a future king, when he returned to Fettes for a second stint Anderson's office was regularly visited by his first future prime minister. 'He was forever knocking at my study door,' he would later recall. 'Round it would come the grinning Blair face, which said, "Sir, I don't think this rule or that rule is right. Can we change it?"' The Shakespearean political drama also continued, with young Anthony Blair taking the role of Mark Antony in *Julius Caesar* dressed in a red toga.

In 1980 Anderson moved to Eton, to teach not one but two future PMs: David Cameron, who described him as one of the most popular headmasters in the school's history, and Boris Johnson, who Anderson said was 'without doubt' the most interesting pupil he had ever had.

Johnson's future modus operandi was clear in his school days. Anderson bumped into him hours before a big essay was due, and he had not even started writing. When it arrived, it was 'very stimulating'. When some students took on a staging of *Richard III*, Johnson – who had the childhood ambition of 'World King' – took the title role. 'He hadn't had time to learn the lines, so had pasted them up behind various pillars,' Anderson told Johnson's biographer Andrew Gimson. 'The whole performance consisted of him running from one side of the stage to the other and failing to read it properly.' A star, and a star's approach to preparation, was born. Other Old Etonians whose dramatic skills were better honed on Anderson's watch include actors Damian Lewis and Dominic West.

Anderson kept on moving. In 1995 he became rector of Lincoln College, Oxford, where one of the students during his time was his fourth future PM. Rishi Sunak was studying philosophy, politics and economics and graduated with a first in 2001, the year after Anderson had returned again to Eton, this time as provost. Having just missed Prince William during his time away at Oxford, he was at Eton for much of Prince Harry's later years as a pupil. During his stints at Eton Anderson combined a traditional conservatism with an understanding of the need to modernise, including abolishing the cane and sending his privileged pupils into poorer inner cities for visits.

Of the many incidents that crossed his many desks during half a century of teaching, there was perhaps none so consequential for the future of politics as the scandal which engulfed Eton in the summer of 1982. 'Seven boys have been expelled from Eton for using cannabis,' *The Daily Telegraph* reported on 3 June 1982. 'They told police that their shared interest in reggae music led them to the London dealers who sold them the drug.' Anderson was quoted as denying that there was any sort of drug ring at the school, insisting that he had 'nipped things in the bud' with the seven expulsions. It could have been – in fact should have been – eight.

As the May 1982 exam season approached, David Cameron was among pupils who had been getting hold of cannabis, 'mostly in the form of hash, typically dark-brown and crumbly, although occasionally some "Red Leb", supposedly from the Bekaa Valley in Lebanon', he revealed years later in his memoirs. He and two friends would take a rowing boat out to an island in the middle of the River Thames with Cameron, as the smallest, acting as the cox. 'Once there, we would roll up and spend a summer's afternoon gently off our heads.'

When the school clamped down on the Eton dealers, his two boating mates were the first to be expelled. Others were caught in the fallout. As time passed, Cameron began to wonder if he might have got away with it. Then he was pulled out of a maths lesson and marched to Anderson's office. There were signed confessions implicating the 15-year-old, whose future now hung in the balance.

Cameron writes that the headmaster sitting behind his desk was in fact the most nervous person in the room, grappling with the language of drug-taking. 'Because I was so keen not to implicate anyone else, I claimed – totally falsely – that I had only smoked cannabis once at Eton, and all the other times were "at home in the village". This involved me telling a more and more elaborate set of lies.' A dumbfounded Anderson asked: 'Yes, Cameron, but who rolled the joint?' More lies followed. 'We were dealing with young boys,' Anderson later told Cameron's biographers Francis Elliott and James Hanning. 'And young boys sometimes do silly things.'

Miraculously, Cameron avoided being thrown out with his fellow pot-smokers. He was fined £20, 'gated', leaving him unable to leave the school's grounds, and made to spend the morning of the school open day on 4 June writing out one of Virgil's *Georgics*. The brush with the law, and the prospect of expulsion, transformed him into a model student in the sixth form that autumn, thriving on history, art and especially economics, where he got a taste for the free marketeers.

Looking back over Anderson's career, the decision to let Cameron off was perhaps the most politically significant. Had he taken a tougher line, or disbelieved his pupil's web of lies, he might only have helped to educate three prime ministers and a king. Which is still not a bad record.

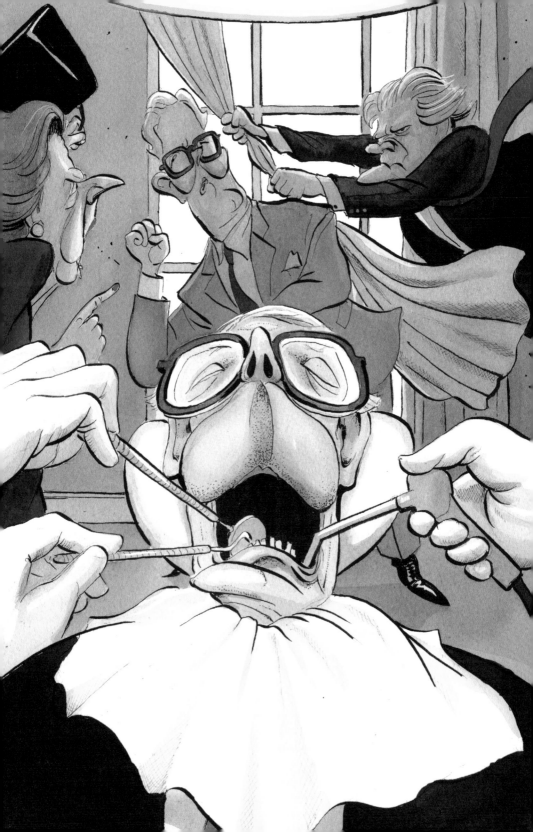

# 7

# John Major's dentist, Bishop's Stortford

*Saturday, 17 November 1990*

'If Halifax had had better teeth,' a pupil declares in Alan Bennett's *The History Boys*, 'we might have lost the war.' It's a good line which captures perfectly the accidental nature of politics. The power of happenstance is strong. It's just that, in this case, it's wrong. The reason why Lord Halifax didn't replace Neville Chamberlain in 1940 is not because he had an appointment at the dentist's the afternoon the decision was made. It was more to do with the fact that he was even less popular with Labour than the guy who got the job of leading the war coalition, Winston Churchill, who, it must be said, was rather less popular with his own colleagues on the Conservative benches. Even so, fifty years later the opposite of the Halifax teeth tale happened – it was a trip to the dentist that helped ease in a new prime minister.

The toothache had been a problem for weeks. Late one night, during a visit to Washington DC, the chancellor had been rushed for emergency treatment on what turned out to be an abscess under a wisdom tooth. The pain was too much. So John Major finally agreed to have it operated on. The problem was, he was going under the dentist's scalpel just as Margaret Thatcher was fighting for her political life. Whether this was terrible timing, or the perfect alibi, was not clear as he succumbed to the anaesthetist's spell.

The seeds of Thatcher's downfall had been sown by the Iron Lady herself: notably the deeply unpopular Poll Tax, which would force everyone to pay a flat rate for local services; and Europe, which had put an increasingly antagonistic and aloof prime minister at odds with her own colleagues. Major had been promoted twice in the space of months, first to replace Geoffrey Howe, who was demoted from foreign secretary to deputy PM in July 1989, and again ninety-four days later to chancellor when Nigel Lawson resigned. It fell to Major to sit silently next to Thatcher on Tuesday, 13 November 1990, while Howe delivered his devastating Commons speech in which he claimed Thatcher's Brussels-bashing had deliberately undermined colleagues. 'It is rather like sending your opening batsmen to the crease,' Howe told a stunned Commons, 'only for them to find, the moment the first balls are bowled, that their bats have been broken before the game by the team captain.' He ended his speech with what was seen as a call to arms to colleagues: 'The time has come for others to consider their own response to the tragic conflict of loyalties, with which I myself have wrestled for perhaps too long.'

Swashbuckling Michael Heseltine, who had quit Thatcher's cabinet in 1986, took his cue, triggering a leadership election by declaring: 'I am persuaded that I would now have a better prospect of leading the Conservatives to a fourth election victory.' In retrospect he might have jumped the gun. Heseltine later told me that actually Howe may have had others in mind: 'I thought when he said "it's now up to others", he was actually thinking about me. Some many years later, in talking to people who were very close to Geoffrey at the time, I was persuaded that he was not referring to me at all, he was referring to the cabinet.' Too late, of course. The race was on.

In the first ballot of Tory MPs on 20 November, Heseltine won 152 votes while Thatcher got 204, a clear majority but 4 votes short of the required margin of 15 per cent. Away at a summit in Paris sketching out a new world order after the Cold War, rather than being at home adding up the numbers, she had blown it. 'I fight on; I fight to win,' she declared. But she wouldn't, she couldn't. A rerun would be worse. The Iron Lady was corroding.

Major missed all this. Having issued a statement urging unity and praising her as 'one of this country's most successful peace-time Prime Ministers', he left London. Three days before the vote, on the morning of Saturday, 17 November 1990, he had opened a fair for Mencap in his Huntingdon constituency, and was then driven by a friend to Herts and Essex Hospital in Bishop's Stortford hoping that the wisdom tooth operation he had booked weeks earlier would finally sort out the pain in his mouth. Thatcher supporters were suspicious of the timing. Why was the new-ish chancellor taking himself out of the action for up to a week just as the prime minister was so vulnerable? Cancel the operation and it would look like panic on behalf of a doomed PM, yet go ahead and raise suspicions of abandoning the boss in her darkest hour. Medical considerations overrode the political – the toothache was too great.

In his autobiography Major recounts the story of waking from the general anaesthetic and being visited by his wife Norma and daughter Elizabeth, when bizarrely they began discussing a tilt at the top job while he was still coming round. 'I remember nothing of the conversation but Elizabeth is certain we talked about whether or not Margaret would make it through the first ballot . . . She says I speculated about whether I should stand. If so, I suspect I was expecting a firm "no" in response. I didn't get it. "Go for it" Elizabeth said. Norma agreed.'

So go for it he did, albeit he was in no position to tell anyone just yet. The sore, gaping hole where the abscess had been meant he could barely speak or eat. His memoirs on this period are striking, if not a little alarming, because while weighing up the life-changing decision on whether to stand to run the country he seems to have been off his head on painkillers. The drug-addled chancellor was 'only half alert' when Norma pointed out the gravity of the prospect of becoming PM. He was, he recalls, 'in no state to talk to anyone for long' as the phone rang off the hook with support for the idea. As the days passed and the crisis deepened, Major was still recuperating at The Finings, the 1930s family home in Great Stukeley near Huntingdon, which was surrounded by high trees, keeping back the press who were by now camped outside. Inside he was, he writes, being 'fed yet more painkillers by Norma'.

After the result was announced Thatcher called her heavily medicated minister and demanded his support by seconding her in the next round of voting. Maybe it was his drugs, maybe it was her directness, but a moment's hesitation before he agreed soured relations between them. Major was still at home when Thatcher famously met her other ministers one by one in the cabinet room, and most said that while of course they personally remained loyal, it was everyone else who was turning against her. On Thursday, 22 November 1990 the triple election winner who reshaped British politics, and Britain itself, was humiliated into withdrawing from the leadership contest that she believed just days earlier she would easily win.

Major finally left The Finings and drove to Westminster, getting snarled up in traffic and making it to his desk at the Treasury with only half an hour to spare before the midday deadline to get his nomination papers in. A clean skin, he could honestly say that all that ghastly business had played out while he had been recuperating, and now here he was ready to run, having obviously done nothing to encourage his own candidacy, what with his teeth. His pitch was simple: he was not Heseltine, the self-styled Tarzan swinging through the Westminster jungle, who had committed the sin of moving against the prime minister. Nor was he Douglas Hurd, whose education at Eton seems to have counted more against him in the Conservative Party of the early 1990s than other Old Etonians found more than a quarter of a century later.

Not that Major was back on top form. Before each public appearance he was again dosed up on antibiotics and paracetamol. Derek Oakley, the husband of Major's constituency secretary Barbara, trailed round after him forcing him to down more 'pills and potions . . . even at one stage leaving them on my pillow, with a despairing note'. On the day of the vote, the impact of both the contest and the operation hit. Mid-afternoon Major took himself off to bed and woke only an hour before the result was announced.

Hurd secured 56 votes and Heseltine 131, with Major way ahead on 185. Not enough to win by the rulebook, but win he obviously had. The rivals soon withdrew. So just ten days after his wisdom tooth operation, John Major stood outside Number 10 as prime minister declaring, somewhat toothily, 'there is a smile on the face of the party' and boasting he would win the next election. Less than eighteen months later he did, securing a surprise victory over Neil Kinnock's Labour with 14,093,007 votes, the most ever cast for any party in a UK general election. Five years of economic and political turmoil later, he would lead the Conservatives to a crushing defeat against Tony Blair's New Labour.

In addition to the convenience of a dental appointment, one of the lasting consequences of this period is the idea that Heseltine lost because he had moved against Thatcher first – despite there being plenty of colleagues who agreed with him at the time. 'He who wields the knife never wears the crown,' Heseltine intoned with characteristic melodrama. In retrospect, this quote is not what it seems. 'I thought I was quoting Shakespeare,' says Heseltine. 'Years later, someone said where did you get that quotation? I said, "Oh I think it's Shakespeare, isn't it?" And they came back to me and said there's no quotation attributed to anybody except you. So I think that maybe it was me originally.'

Maybe it was being the sort of person who would quote himself believing it to be Shakespeare that counted against him. Maybe if Major had been in Westminster, not in a drug-induced fug at home, he too would have been tainted, as either the favoured heir or unfaithful assassin. Politics is a lot of maybes. Recent political history is littered with ditherers who hoped to obtain the crown while hoping someone else would do the dirty work – just ask David Miliband or Penny Mordaunt. Yet Gordon Brown spent a decade doing a lot of wielding while Tony Blair was in Number 10 before taking the crown himself. Boris Johnson's weapon was rarely sheathed. Even Rishi Sunak, who was initially punished by Tory members for knifing Johnson in the summer of 2022, got there in the end. And if Major had had better teeth, he might have lost the keys to Number 10.

# Bathrooms

# 8

# Patrick Jenkin's toothbrush, Highgate

*Tuesday, 15 January 1974*

People power is important. And anyone who tries to take power from the people should expect an electric shock. In early 1974 Britain was in the grip of the miners' strike, with a lack of coal limiting power generation. Edward Heath's government had imposed the three-day week, curtailing businesses from using electricity the rest of the time. TV broadcasts shut down at 10.30 p.m. The pubs were closed. Grim times.

By mid-January it was clear that only seeking to reduce the energy use of big business was not working. The government had set a target of a 25 per cent cut in electricity demand, but was struggling to hit even 15 per cent. Ministers were considering changing the law to make it illegal to have the lights on in more than one room at once, sparking a national debate about how it might work in practice. 'Would anyone going to the lavatory have to ensure that everyone else in the house was sitting in the dark?' *The Guardian* asked. There was talk of policemen having to knock on any homes with 'lights ablaze'. TV adverts told families to SOS – 'Switch Off Something – Now'.

Patrick Jenkin, the immaculately dressed, newly appointed energy minister, had a not-so-bright idea. A politician who probably belonged to an earlier, less media-focused age, on 15 January

1974 he went on BBC Radio 1's *Newsbeat* and urged households to do more to cut electricity use: 'People can clean their teeth in the dark, use the top of the stove instead of the oven, all sorts of savings, but they must use less electricity.'

It conjured up an unfortunate image of the minister alone in his bathroom brushing his teeth in pitch-black. Normally a politician gets into trouble for what they get up to when they are not in their pyjamas. But the backlash was swift and brutal. Reports went around the world of Brits brushing their teeth but finding themselves using 'shaving cream and other tubed concoctions rather than toothpaste'.

It is never wise for a politician in hot water to drag the family into it – think John Gummer's daughter eating a BSE-free burger – but Jenkin fell into exactly that trap. The front page of *The Daily Telegraph* carried a large photograph with the caption: 'An automatic dishwasher standing idle as Mrs Monica Jenkin, wife of the new Minister of Energy, washed up by hand last night, assisted by her daughter, Flora, 12, as part of her "terrific" campaign to save electricity at their Highgate home. The refrigerator has been switched off and the gas central heating turned down.' In the cash-strapped early seventies few homes had an 'automatic dishwasher', idle or otherwise. Jenkin himself then posed for the cameras shaving by candlelight but hilariously using an electric razor. An even less successful snap emerged when a photographer took a picture of the Jenkin abode, with the porch light on and every room well lit. 'They must have caught us at a bad moment,' Mrs Jenkin, taking a break from the washing up, confessed. Days later Jenkin admitted his mistake. 'The press are right and the suggestion I made on radio the other day was not a practical one.'

It is a brave politician indeed who tries to tell hard-pressed families how to light and warm their homes. Just a few years later, in 1977, Jimmy Carter appeared on TV shortly after becoming US president to urge the country to make sacrifices and save energy. 'All of us must learn to waste less energy. Simply by keeping our thermostats, for instance, at 65 degrees in the daytime and 55 degrees at night we could save half the current shortage of natural gas.' He did so in a woolly cardigan, which was seen as terribly insensitive attire in which to lecture the nation.

In 2013 David Cameron did the same thing. Or didn't. Gas companies were hiking bills, and Ed Davey, the Lib Dem energy secretary in the coalition, had been on BBC 2's *Newsnight* and outrageously confided: 'I am sure people do wear jumpers, I wear jumpers at home.' At the lobby briefing the next day, a Friday, bored journalists demanded answers about whether Cameron also wore a woolly, teasing officials with increasingly absurd questions. Did the PM wear a jumper at home? 'The prime minister doesn't tend to give fashion tips,' the relatively new official spokesman replied. On and on it went, dancing around the prime minister's position on pullovers. Until, finally, the spokesman cracked. 'Clearly, he is not going to prescribe necessarily the actions individuals should take about that,' he began, before adding: 'But . . . that is something that people may wish to consider.'

All hell broke loose. The posh PM lecturing the poor on what to wear. No greater authority on energy policy than *Britain's Got Talent* winner Susan Boyle joined the outcry, telling *The Sun*: 'I found it inconceivable that the man running the country – who should be looking out and protecting the people of the UK – would turn around and tell the nation to wear a jumper when the energy companies announced vast price rises.'

Downing Street then issued the laughable statement: 'To be clear, it is entirely false to suggest the prime minister would advise people they should wear jumpers to stay warm.' What? Why wouldn't he? Is it government policy that jumpers don't keep you warm? The whole episode was a pretty terrible example of the way the lobby sometimes works, and how stating the bleeding obvious can get you into trouble. 'It can be funny,' says Sir Craig Oliver, who was the Number 10 director of communication at the time. 'But that guy lost his job because of it.'

In 2022, following the Russian invasion of Ukraine, energy prices again spiked and politicians again panicked about whether to launch an advertising campaign to tell people how to save money on their bills. Graham Stuart, the climate minister, declined: 'We're not a nanny state government.' Ironically it was Jacob Rees-Mogg, the only member of the government to have gone campaigning with his nanny, who was in favour of the idea as business secretary but was overruled by Liz Truss. In the end she lost power before the homes of Britain did.

# 9

# Margaret Thatcher's bathroom, Brighton

*Friday, 12 October 1984*

A piece of paper saved Margaret Thatcher's life. After a long day and night working on her party conference speech, the prime minister was about to go into her bathroom on the first floor of the Grand Hotel in Brighton and prepare for bed. Robin Butler, her principal private secretary, had just one more piece of paper for her to take a look at, as principal private secretaries often do.

At 2.54 a.m. an IRA bomb went off, ripping through the white, wedding cake façade of the seafront hotel, intended to kill the prime minister and her cabinet. *The Telegraph*'s David Hughes called it 'the most audacious attack on a British government since the Gunpowder Plot'. Five people died: Sir Anthony Berry, MP for Enfield and Southgate; Eric Taylor, chairman of the North-West area Conservatives; Jeanne Shattock, wife of the South-West chairman Sir Gordon Shattock; Muriel Maclean, wife of Scottish Conservatives president Sir Donald Maclean; and Roberta Wakeham, wife of chief whip John Wakeham. Among the injured were Norman Tebbit, the trade and industry secretary, and his wife, Margaret, who was paralysed from the chest down and spent the rest of her life in a wheelchair.

Four weeks earlier a man called Roy Walsh had checked into the Grand for four nights, staying in room 629, enjoying the last days of summer. In fact he was Patrick Magee, a member of the Provisional IRA opposed to British rule in Northern Ireland, and he planted a 20lb gelignite bomb and timer behind the bath panel in his room.

A month later Thatcher and her husband Denis moved into the Napoleon suite five floors below. The prime minister had spent the day listening to conference debates, meeting Tory officials and lunching with women party chairmen from across the country. Every spare moment was used to frantically work on her leader's speech. After popping into a ball for party agents, at 11.15 p.m. she returned to the Grand Hotel for more speechwriting.

A little after 2.30 a.m. she finished working in the sitting room of the suite and handed the last page to two of her staff. She told them after a long day that they should go to bed. Then Butler appeared and said: 'I know you are tired, but there is just one more paper you must do because they want the answer tomorrow.' So the PM sat down again and began reading a memo about the Liverpool Garden Festival. 'That was when the bomb went off,' she recalled to *Woman's Own* a month later. 'The window and the curtain blew out, blew out into the street. There was a great whoosh of air and dust. I stood up and went towards the bedroom, but Denis was already coming out.'

It had been reported, incorrectly, that she had been in the bathroom moments before the blast. 'I would have been if Robin had not asked me to look at the final paper,' she said. Part of the bathroom ceiling had come down, the floor around the toilet, bidet and bath was covered in rubble, large shards of glass hanging in the window. Anyone who had been in there at the time would have been seriously injured, or worse. 'Those who had sought to kill me had placed the bomb in the wrong place,' Thatcher later wrote in her memoirs, *The Downing Street Years*. In fact it was probably in the right place, it was luck rather than error which saved her.

There was a struggle to get out of the hotel. Her throat thick with cement dust, and still wearing the gown and pearls from the ball, the prime minister clambered over broken furniture and discarded belongings to get to the back entrance. Within minutes she was whisked away to Brighton police station, spent what was left of the night at Lewes Police Training College, and returned to the Brighton centre at 9 a.m., where the conference began with a two-minute silence and then, incredibly, continued as normal.

At just after 2.30 p.m. Thatcher addressed the party, and the country: 'The bomb attack on the Grand Hotel early this morning was first and foremost an inhuman, undiscriminating attempt to massacre innocent, unsuspecting men and women staying in Brighton for our Conservative Conference. Our first thoughts must at once be for those who died and for those who are now in hospital recovering from their injuries.

'But the bomb attack clearly signified more than this. It was an attempt not only to disrupt and terminate our conference; it was an attempt to cripple Her Majesty's democratically elected government. That is the scale of the outrage in which we have all shared, and the fact that we are gathered here now – shocked, but composed and determined – is a sign not only that this attack has failed, but that all attempts to destroy democracy by terrorism will fail.'

She turned the page, and returned to the speech that she had stuffed into a briefcase in the minutes after the bomb had gone off. 'And now it must be business as usual,' she said, going on to discuss foreign policy, unemployment and the miners' strike, while dropping some of the overtly political attacks on her Labour opponents.

Yet so much else had changed. Tentative, secret steps towards a solution in Northern Ireland were set back. '"The bomb" has slowed things down,' Thatcher wrote in a prime ministerial note to officials. Thatcher herself was changed too. She wrote in her memoirs of the 'deceptive normality' in the moments after the blast. 'The lights, thankfully, remained on: the importance of this played on my mind for some time and for months after-wards I always kept a torch by my bed when I was staying the night in a strange house.'

Politics changed too. Party conferences in particular became an increasingly high-security affair. Today a ring of steel is thrown around the annual gatherings of the main parties. Sniffer dogs tour the perimeter, watched by snipers from the rooftops. There are barcoded lanyards to be checked, X-ray scanners for every bag and coat. In 2007 there was uproar at the Lib Dem conference in Brighton when a councillor was stopped from entering because she was carrying a dangerous weapon. A pair of knitting needles.

# 10

# Nick Ryden's toilet, Edinburgh

*Monday, 16 May 1994*

Tony Blair sat and waited. And waited. And waited. Alone in the front room of the Edinburgh home of his old school friend Nick Ryden, Blair jumped as the telephone began to ring. It not being his house, he let the answering machine take it. 'Tony,' a voice boomed from the box in the corner. 'It's Gordon here.' At this, Blair was a little freaked out. 'I am upstairs in the toilet and I can't get out.'

Ryden was a property developer and was in the process of doing up a rambling mansion in Merchiston, a posh suburb of Edinburgh. A new door on the bathroom had not had its inside handle fitted. Gordon Brown's vocal cries for help had gone unanswered. For more than fifteen minutes he had been using his big brick of a mobile to call round friends and colleagues to get hold of Ryden's landline number. (Blair did not have a mobile – and wouldn't get one until after he left Downing Street.) When Blair finally climbed the stairs to rescue his colleague, he had an ultimatum, shouting through the door: 'Withdraw from the contest or I'm leaving you in there.'

It was four days after the death of John Smith, the 55-year-old Labour leader, had been announced. It would be another four days before he would be laid to rest, but politics is a brutal business and before he was in the ground on the beautiful Hebridean island of Iona, attention was already turning to who would replace him. Brown as shadow chancellor was clearly the senior partner over Blair, then shadow home secretary, or at least he thought so.

During the previous decade, while toiling on the back benches, whenever the question of leadership had come up Blair had repeatedly told Brown that he would back him. Brown claims that Blair had told him he did not want to be leader, and might even leave politics for TV. Blair admits that he had spent the past two years being 'disingenuous' with Brown, giving him assurances that he would support him, presuming it would never come to pass because Smith would go on to be prime minister.

And then Smith died, suffering a heart attack at his London flat on Thursday, 12 May 1994. Blair had apparently predicted this. In his memoirs he recalls spending a few days in Paris with his wife Cherie in April 1994. He woke on the first morning and told her: 'If John dies, I will be leader. And somehow, I think this will happen. I just think it will.' And when the first part came true, he moved quickly to secure part two. Brown, who spent those first days writing obituaries and tributes, might decry the unseemly haste, but that's politics. By that first weekend after Smith's death newspaper articles and TV debate shows were dominated by the apparent inevitability of a Blair victory.

Brown decided that a public battle would harm the party, that they could not stand against each other, that someone would have to give way. Blair, meanwhile, had decided that that someone had to be Brown, resolving to 'cajole' him out of the race early rather than have to confront and defeat him head on. So began a series of clandestine meetings at the homes of friends of Blair, an early indication of who had the upper hand. These conversations were held variously at the Rydens' home in Edinburgh, at Blair's sister-in-law's in Richmond Crescent in London and, most oddly, at an Edinburgh flat belonging to the parents of Blair's former girlfriend and first love, Amanda Mackenzie Stuart.

It was at the latter that, according to Blair anyway, Brown first acknowledged the possibility that he would not stand. After that it was just a case of managing his withdrawal from the race. Which is what they were discussing at chez Ryden, while the homeowner was banished to the local pub. There was wine, whisky and an

Indian takeaway. After being rescued from the bathroom, Brown stayed late thrashing out the future direction of a Blair-led Labour Party and his role in it. Ryden was finally told he could come home at 1.30 a.m. The deal had been done.

Brown claims that in the days after Smith's death, Blair not only promised him that he could stay as shadow chancellor but that he would also have control of economic and social policy. Blair insists he himself would always remain in charge, and bristles at the idea that he was an empty vessel into which Brown would simply pour his big ideas. More significantly, Brown claims that Blair promised he would stand down as PM in his second term to spend time with his children, who would by then be in their teens. 'It was a promise he repeated on several occasions,' Brown wrote in his memoirs. Blair in his own account is a little more oblique, without actually denying it: 'Had you asked me then what I would do and what might happen, I would have said I would do two terms and then hand over.' Wisely, or otherwise, Brown took Blair at his word. Or perhaps recognised the reality that he could not actually win a leadership contest. Either way, he conceded he would not stand in 1994, finally telling those closest to him of his decision in the last days of May. 'The rest was a formality,' he wrote in his memoirs.

'The rest', of course, was the dinner at Granita. This modish Mediterranean restaurant in north London was perhaps the most obvious location for inclusion in a collection of places which changed politics, were it not for the fact that it didn't. Granita was not where a deal was made, but it was where the fate of both men, and the country, was sealed. Blair was the first to arrive at Granita on the evening of Tuesday, 30 May 1994. He already knew he was going to be Labour leader. Like the venues for the earlier talks, he had also chosen the restaurant, with its fashionable stripped wooden floors and bare white walls. The absence of tablecloths and – heavens! – fish knives was the talk of the town. And could not have been less Gordon Brown, the parsimonious son of the manse.

Brown was not looking forward to the meal, when the main thing he would have to swallow was his pride, so invited along Ed Balls, a 27-year-old former *Financial Times* journalist who just three months earlier had become his economic adviser. Balls's first job was to tell the maître d' 'We're here to see Tony Blair', to spare Brown from even having to utter the words. They walked the length of the narrow restaurant to find Blair sitting alone off to the right at a table set for two. Brown made a great fuss, insisting on a third chair and menu for Balls, who tells me that his boss looked at the menu in horror: 'The first thing he does, having acknowledged Tony's existence, is he turns to me and says: "What exactly is polenta?" I'm pretty sure that Tony had chipirones, you know, baby octopus.' Having successfully chaperoned Brown to the table, Balls left, so did not hear if Blair repeated the commitment, vague or otherwise, that he might stand down after two terms. 'He may have foolishly said that, in a speculative way, and Gordon may have foolishly believed him', Balls says now.

On the way out Balls clocked another diner, the journalist Allison Pearson, and realised that any hope of the meeting staying secret was futile. However, Pearson says that 'all the excitement was caused by the presence of Susan Tully, who played Michelle in *EastEnders*. No one gave the historic summit a second glance.' In truth, in 1994 the Blair/Brown soap opera was not gripping the attention of millions. At least not yet. Pearson adds that Granita was 'very Islington, very uncomfortable for Brown. Light wood floors, clattery, open, small tables, hopeless place for a clandestine meeting. So maybe someone didn't care for it to be secret . . .'

Leaving the restaurant barely an hour later, Blair was full of talk of 'partnership', but Brown's mind was on more pressing matters – some proper food. Four miles away, Balls was waiting with spin doctor Charlie Whelan at the Rodin restaurant in Millbank, a short walk across the street from Parliament. Balls's mobile phone rang. It was Brown: 'Well done steak and chips, please.' Clearly he had found the Mediterranean fare even less palatable than the topic of conversation. When Brown arrived, attention quickly turned to the future and what happened next. 'It was neither dour, nor celebratory,' says Balls. 'It was kind of operational, professional.'

Overnight Brown began drafting the text of what would be briefed to the press about the outcome of the secret meetings in Edinburgh, although even this was not without problems. So many redrafts were sent between the rival camps that Peter Mandelson, acting as a broker between the two, had to send someone into Hartlepool to buy a replacement fax when his home machine broke down. There was no mention in the text of timescales or standing down, and even on policy it was vague. In 2003 *The Guardian* published one version which stated that Blair was 'in full agreement with' Brown's agenda on social justice, employment and skills, but Brown crossed this out and wrote more firmly that Blair 'has guaranteed this will be pursued'. This painstaking process would form the basis of how they would come to operate in government, with Blair and Brown, and warring aides, tweaking texts until both camps were happy, or at least equally unhappy.

At 3.30 p.m. on Wednesday, 1 June 1994 Brown released his statement confirming he was withdrawing from the leadership race. New Labour, led by Blair, went on to win a landslide 179-seat majority in 1997, and Blair's deadline, such as it was, to stand down in the second term came and went. In 2004 he actually vowed to serve a full third term, but not a fourth. In fact he managed barely a year after the 2005 election before Brown's patience ran out, and he finally stood down in June 2007.

Granita had an even more troubled time. It closed in 2003, becoming first a restaurant called Desperados, then an estate agents in 2013. That lasted barely three years, before standing empty as a developer's showroom before, in 2022, opening as a women's clothes and interiors store. 'The restaurant did not survive,' Brown wrote. 'And ultimately neither did our agreement.'

I once asked Blair, more than twenty-five years after Nick Ryden's toilet and Granita and all of that, if he wished with hindsight that he had tried to sort out the relationship with Brown properly before going into government. 'I don't think it was sortable in the end,' he said. 'Because it was born of what was a very difficult passage when John Smith died and then I became leader. But certainly at that stage, whatever difficulties there were, were more than compensated by the enormous contribution that Gordon made. But I think the essence of the problem was never . . . never really changed.' Perhaps, in the end, he should have left him in the toilet.

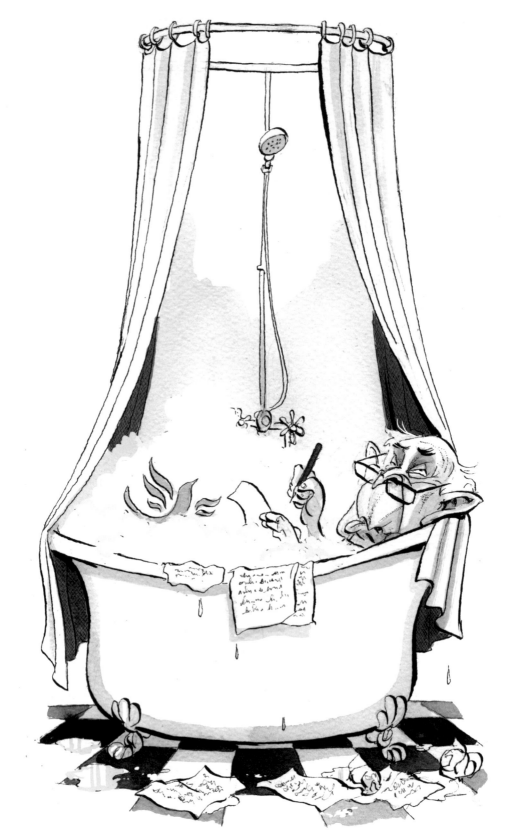

# 11

# Vince Cable's bath, Twickenham

*Tuesday, 27 November 2008*

There are few greater sentences to hear from a spin doctor than 'How did you find out about that?' In their rush to express shock, or even anger, they also provide confirmation that the story is true. I went to the 2017 Lib Dem conference in Bournemouth expecting my only scoop to be vanilla on a cone with a flake. But I kept hearing that magic phrase: 'How did you find out about that?'

What I had found out was that there were naked photos in circulation of the party's then leader, Sir Vince Cable. Quite the mental image. The pictures were of the 74-year-old in the bath and were apparently taken by his wife, Rachel, who had sent them for printing. Cable had been recognised by someone doing the processing, the pictures passed through various hands before ending up on the desk of at least one Sunday newspaper, and then finding their way back to a Lib Dem press officer. 'There are some things you can't unsee,' was how one person described the snaps, explaining that a combination of the photographic angle and a plentiful supply of bubbles mercifully meant that the right honourable member was obscured below the waterline. The papers decided that nobody wanted to see that over their breakfast and declined to print them.

Yet the Cable bathtub has a special place in British politics. The one-time Shell executive and economist did much of his political thinking while having a soak. And on the evening of Tuesday, 27 November 2008 he was in his bath trying to come up with some lines for Prime Minister's Questions the next day. Some politicians rely on vast teams to brainstorm clever-clever strategies. Not Cable. Something of a loner even in his own party, he would turn up to the Commons most days having already decided what he would say.

In November 2007 Gordon Brown had been prime minister for five months. He initially surged in the polls on replacing Tony Blair, in part thanks to sure-footed responses to a terror attack, floods and a foot-and-mouth outbreak. His appeal was summed up in a Saatchi & Saatchi ad campaign pitching him as 'Not flash, just Gordon', the antidote to his predecessor's PR sheen. But he then bottled calling a general election in September, and his popularity plunged faster than shares in Northern Rock. Everything he touched seemed to go wrong. The banking system he had presided over as chancellor now teetered on the brink. HM Revenue and Customs lost the confidential details of 9 million adults and 15 million children. Ministers twice had to admit they had underestimated how many foreign workers were in the country. And then Labour became embroiled in a donations scandal, with allegations that property tycoon David Abrahams had given the party £600,000 through go-betweens, including his builder and secretary, to remain anonymous. Brown, who had vowed to restore trust just months after a police investigation into political funding had dogged the last days of Blair's government, set up not one but two inquiries into his own party's finances. In the end no charges were brought and Abrahams was ultimately cleared.

A month earlier Cable had become acting Lib Dem leader, following the resignation of Sir Menzies Campbell after months of criticism about his performance (and age – despite being only two years older than Cable). This was back in the days when the Lib Dems had enough MPs to be the third-largest party in Westminster, and therefore have two questions guaranteed at Prime Minister's Questions. After David Cameron had enjoyed himself by mercilessly, if unmemorably, mocking 'disaster after disaster', leaving Brown squirming over donations, Cable rose to his feet against the background noise of sarcastic cheers from the bigger parties. He was ready to deliver his bath bomb:

'Mr Speaker, the er . . . the House has noticed the Prime Minister's remarkable transformation in the last few weeks from . . . Stalin to Mr Bean.' The House of Commons collapsed into a rare thing: genuine laughter. Giddy Tim Farron, a Lib Dem MP, nearly fell off the bench behind Cable. The laughter went on for more than ten seconds, crescendoing in loud cheers. Cable's decent follow-up line – that Brown was 'creating chaos out of order, rather than order out of chaos' – didn't get the same response, but it didn't matter. Similarly, almost nobody in the Commons chamber that day, or the press gallery where I was sitting, will easily recall what Cable's question was actually about. In fact, he went on to raise concerns from forces chiefs who had accused Brown of 'wilfully neglecting the safety and welfare of the young men and women who serve in our armed forces'. All that is lost to *Hansard* and history. The long-soak one-liner had done its job.

After initially coming up with the Stalin/Bean jibe in the bath, Cable had tried it out on Rachel, who told him: 'Oh no, I don't think so.' Too knockabout, too silly, too school playground. He ignored her, egged on by his political team, who thought it was funny. It worked. It went viral at a time when nobody really knew what going viral meant, reaching wide audiences online. In October 2007, 38 per cent of people had told Ipsos MORI they were dissatisfied with Brown as prime minister. A few days after Stalin/Bean that had jumped to 54 per cent. We can argue about cause and effect, but there is no doubt that Cable had captured the public mood with his bath-time soundbite.

A few months later, in an interview with the *New Statesman*, Brown sidestepped the Mr Bean talk and compared himself instead to 'an older Heathcliff, a wiser Heathcliff', the dark and brooding character created by Emily Brontë. His reputation never recovered, though, and he was unable to recapture his early wuthering heights in the polls, as his personal ratings disappeared down the plughole.

*Furniture*

# 12

# Gladstone's chair, Liverpool

*October 1812*

Even on a cloudy day in Liverpool, 62 Rodney Street is an imposing building. Three storeys high (four including the basement), five windows wide, five steps up to a jet-black door framed by smart cream pillars and portico. The multiple doorbells are the giveaway that this grand old family home has, inevitably, been carved into flats. The grey plaque set into the wall is the only hint of what occurred here when it was a single dwelling: 'Gladstone. Four times prime minister. Born in this house 29th December 1809.' And one October evening less than three years later, a political career would be born here too. One of Britain's greatest and most influential prime ministers first got a taste for politics at the age of 2, and barely twenty years later he was an MP.

Gladstone's father, John, was a merchant and slave owner who would become an MP before his son. Gladstone Snr was a close ally of George Canning, who would fifteen years later become prime minister (albeit only briefly), and would often pop by. Gladstone junior wrote in his memoirs that one of his earliest memories was of a visit by Canning to Rodney Street in October 1812: 'Much entertaining went on in my father's house, where Mr. Canning himself was a guest; and on a day of a great dinner I was taken down to the dining room. I was set upon one of the chairs, standing, and directed to say to the company "Ladies and gentlemen".'

Those three words, calling order in a rowdy dining room, were in effect Gladstone's first speech, at the tender age of just two. From there he certainly got a taste for it, securing a reputation later in life for his ability to speak at extraordinary length. President of the Oxford Union, he gained a double first in mathematics and classics, complaining that his oral exam was too easy. When the examiner tried to change the subject, Gladstone replied: 'No, sir; if you please, we will not leave it yet' and carried on talking. His sprawling political career meant there was plenty of time for speeches: first elected as an MP aged 22, he finally stood down as prime minister for the fourth time sixty years later. It was quite a journey: beginning his career as a Tory in Newark, he was as reactionary as they came, defending his father's ownership of slaves, before softening many of his earlier positions and becoming a great parliamentary reformer, anti-imperialist and tax-cutter. His early public speaking as an MP caught the eye of Robert Peel, who gave him his first junior ministerial post. When the Tory Party split in 1846 over trade, Gladstone followed Peel in joining what became the Liberal Party.

The near-verbatim newspaper reproduction of his many speeches over six decades in politics no doubt cost more trees than even he felled during his strange recreational habit of taking an axe into the woods. In a landmark 1850 parliamentary debate on the principles of British foreign policy he spoke for three hours solid. In December 1852, the Tory chancellor Benjamin Disraeli took two and a half hours to wind up a debate on his first Budget. It was 1 a.m., and most present were ready to go home. Not Gladstone, who went on to spend the next two hours verbally shredding it, fuelling his great rivalry with Disraeli. Within days the minority Tory government fell and Gladstone took Disraeli's job in the coalition of Peelites and Whigs formed under Lord Aberdeen. Gladstone's first Budget speech as chancellor in April 1853 lasted more than four hours and forty-five minutes. (It included scrapping 123 duties and cutting 133 others, but his promise to abolish income tax remains unfulfilled to this day.) On and on he went, becoming prime minister for the first time in 1868. His resignation speech after losing the 1874 election lasted a mere ninety minutes, but that's perhaps ten times longer than the valedictories on the steps of Number 10 we get these days.

It was the speeches delivered in the run-up to the 1880 election which had the most lasting impact on politics as we know it today. Gladstone had given up his Greenwich seat, and was persuaded to stand in the area around Edinburgh. The Midlothian campaign saw the 70-year-old mount a spirited challenge against the Tory aristocratic incumbent Lord Dalkeith, delivering a series of barnstorming speeches across Scotland, mostly condemning Disraeli's foreign policy. 'It comes to this,' he said of the overstretched British forces, 'that you are increasing your engagements without increasing your strength; and if you increase your engagements without increasing strength, you diminish strength, you abolish strength; you really reduce the empire and do not increase it.'

The target audience of the speeches was not the tens of thousands who filled town halls, corn exchanges and train station platforms to hear him. It was the many more who would read detailed accounts of them in the daily papers. It meant Gladstone, who spoke off the cuff with minimal preparation, had to work hard to make the content and colour sufficiently different to be worth reporting each day. It was, in many ways, the model for election campaigning even today. It worked: when the Liberals won a landslide victory in January 1880, the party's nominal leaders Lord Hartington and Lord Granville had little option but to give way to Gladstone, who was credited at the time with helping to secure the win. He was PM this time until 1885, returned briefly in 1886, and ran again in 1892. During that election campaign an incident occurred which summed up his extraordinary appeal. Campaigning in Chester, a large crowd had gathered when someone hurled something at the prime minister. It hit him in the eye. It turned out to be a hard gingerbread nut biscuit.

For the rest of the campaign Gladstone had to wear dark glasses. But this was not a protest. According to a letter sent to *The Times* a few days later, 'the lady who threw the gingerbread at him in Chester is one of his most ardent supporters. Far from intending to insult him, she only attempted to give some outward expression of her frenzied admiration'. Gladstone won the election, and remained in office as PM until 1894. His ministers burst into tears in cabinet on the news of his final resignation.

His speeches were notable for not patronising his audience, instead treating them to lectures of the same complexity, and length, as if he were in the Commons chamber. Long, if not rambling then sub-clause-strewn, sentences which would have fallen flat or lost an audience in a lesser mouth instead soared and captured the imagination. It did not always come easy, though, with Gladstone occasionally writing in his diaries of nervousness, especially when made to wait for long periods before being called to speak in Commons debates.

Nor did everyone enjoy the sound of his voice as much as he did. Disraeli once dismissed him as 'a sophistical rhetorician, inebriated with the exuberance of his own verbosity, and gifted with an egotistical imagination that can at all times command an interminable and inconsistent series of arguments to malign an opponent and to glorify himself'. Queen Victoria was pithier in her putdown: 'He addresses me as though I were a public meeting.'

Quite what she would have made of the lacklustre sophistry of today's politicians we can only imagine. But Gladstone created the modern election campaign as we know it, with carefully crafted messages, delivered again and again to enraptured crowds, repeated by the media to the masses. And he first got a taste for it on a dining-room chair aged two.

These days Liverpool's Rodney Street is known as the 'Harley Street of the North', with many of the townhouses now the offices of cosmetic surgeons. Beneath the old street sign is an advert for a firm selling skin peels, lashes and fillers. A beauty salon and training academy offers make-up training, aesthetics 'and more'. There is a lazy pun to be had about how this is fitting for the birthplace of a man who changed the face of British politics. But I shall not stoop to use it.

# 13

# Salisbury's sofa, Downing Street

*Wednesday, 12 January 1887*

Stafford Northcote's problem is that he was too nice. He should have been prime minister. Instead, the most notable thing he did in 10 Downing Street was to drop dead while waiting to be officially sacked in a ruthless reshuffle carried out by his party colleague, who had beaten him to become PM. Number 10's role as a place which has changed politics has been well told elsewhere. It has been the location of momentous meetings, decisive (and often indecisive) decisions, of late nights and early mornings, high politics and low skulduggery from its inception as the prime minister's official residence in 1775 to this day. Yet no serving prime minister has died there (seven expired elsewhere while in office), so a death in Downing Street is more notable than the routine machinations that you might expect.

Nothing better illustrates how politics is, and always has been, a rough business than the manner in which Northcote died: prone on a sofa in the anteroom of the man who was once his junior but took the role of prime minister that could rightly have been his. There is an enormous, if almost entirely ignored, statue of Northcote and his fine beard in the central lobby of the Houses of Parliament, a monument guiltily erected by those he left behind, and a cautionary tale to all who pass it obliviously today.

Northcote was born into a Devon country family in 1818, and studied classics at Oxford before being called to the Bar. In his mid-twenties he was hired as a private secretary by William Gladstone, who was then president of the Board of Trade in the Conservative government of Robert Peel. Northcote worked on the Great Exhibition of 1851, and later with Sir Charles Trevelyan drew up the Northcote–Trevelyan Report, the founding of the modern, impartial civil service as we know it, 'able to transfer its loyalty and expertise from one elected government to the next'. Northcote was probably a better impartial official than hard-nosed politician. Working together for some nine years, Northcote and Gladstone became close friends. However, when Gladstone joined the breakaway Peelite split, eventually ending up in the Liberal Party, Northcote remained with the Conservatives, rising through the party's ranks under Benjamin Disraeli. 'Northcote managed the most unusual feat of admiring both Gladstone and Disraeli,' notes Lord Lexden, the official historian of the Conservative Party.

During three decades in politics, Northcote held some of the biggest government jobs in Victorian Britain: president of the Board of Trade, secretary of state for India and a well-regarded spell as a tax-cutting chancellor of the exchequer. Then, in 1876, when Disraeli went to the House of Lords, apparently in search of a quieter life, he remained as prime minister but left Northcote as Tory leader in the Commons, a job for which, unfortunately, he was spectacularly ill suited. In part it was because it meant going up against Gladstone, his old mentor, who was now Liberal leader of the Opposition across the despatch box. This, critics at the time claimed, weakened his lines of attack, if not paralysed them. 'He was mild in temperament,' *The Times* wrote after his death: 'Judicial in disposition, gentle in demeanour, courteous to opponents, slow to take offence, slower still to give it.' Exactly the sort of person the public often wants in politics, but who turns out to be spectacularly bad at politics. Northcote himself once admitted that he was deficient in 'go'.

When the Liberals won the 1880 election and Gladstone became prime minister for the second time, Northcote struggled even more as leader of the opposition in the Commons, failing to capitalise on the government's woes. When Disraeli died he was replaced as the Tory leader in the Lords by Lord Salisbury. There was no single Conservative leader in opposition until 1922, but in theory Northcote, having been in post for longer, had seniority. In practice, Salisbury and his supporters were growing fed up with Mr Nice Guy.

In the 1885 election Gladstone's Liberals lost their majority, but the Conservatives fell short of an outright win. Queen Victoria did not send for Northcote to be prime minister as he had expected, and probably deserved. Instead, Salisbury, more of a political bruiser, got the job, and would go on to spend thirteen and a half of the next seventeen years as prime minister. The snub was humiliating for Northcote, who was 'kicked upstairs' and sent to the Lords himself as the Earl of Iddesleigh. At another general election in 1886, Salisbury won a decent majority and he made Northcote his foreign secretary – a job Salisbury had held himself with distinction. A tough gig doing your boss's old job, and Northcote again failed to live up to expectations, ill-health meaning he was no longer the man he once was.

Within months rumours appeared in the press that Northcote would be sacked. Soon it became clear that Salisbury was to embark on what has since become a political tradition: a new-year reshuffle. A cabinet meeting had been expected on Tuesday, 5 January, but Salisbury was still trying to finalise the reshuffle so it was delayed until the following weekend. The papers were cruelly briefed that Northcote was 'ready to retire in order to facilitate Lord Salisbury's reconstruction of his cabinet'. A lovely euphemism for being sacked. It was also suggested that he might be offered 'some post of dignity, the duties of which are lighter than those he is now relinquishing'. So he was getting the sack and a consolation prize. The meeting of the new cabinet was delayed again. Trouble was brewing. As the days passed, it was claimed that the Conservative rank and file felt no effort should be spared to induce Northcote to stay in the cabinet. One colleague even offered to give up his cabinet seat for him. In fact, Salisbury had decided to simply appoint himself foreign secretary as well as being PM.

On Wednesday, 12 January 1887, after more than a fortnight of being briefed against, Northcote knew the game was up. He went back to the Foreign Office for a meeting with the celebrated explorer Henry Morton Stanley, but asked for it to be rearranged for 6 o'clock that evening. On the way out he spoke to Sir James Ferguson, a junior Foreign Office minister, who later recalled Northcote expressing a hope that his exile from government might not be permanent. 'He was looking as well as, or better than, usual,' Ferguson said. After having lunch, Northcote made the short walk from the Foreign Office across to Downing Street at 2.45 p.m. He struggled to make it breathlessly up the stairs to the prime minister's offices on the first floor. A messenger was sent to tell Salisbury that he had a visitor; Northcote was to wait in an anteroom. He sank into the nearest chair by the door. When the messenger returned and called him to come through, instead of getting up Northcote said between groans: 'I will be with Lord Salisbury in a minute.' His anguished cries attracted the attention of Henry Manners, the prime minister's secretary, who was in the next room and rushed in just in time to catch Northcote as he fell from his chair. Doctors were sent for, and Northcote was moved to a sofa, his tie and collar loosened. Salisbury rushed in. Attempts to revive Northcote failed. After two final gasps, he died. He was 68.

In its obituary *The Times* wrote that Northcote was 'the man of perfect courtesy of soul, the man who by word, deed and conduct always strove to make others content with themselves and with him'. Queen Victoria mentioned Northcote's death in her personal diary: 'He fainted at the top of the stairs at Downing Street,' she wrote, 'and he died in twenty minutes. I felt quite bewildered and stunned.' Less surprised were his own oft-consulted doctors, who said it was 'not unforeseen by his immediate friends, and had been anticipated by his medical attendants'. In a letter Salisbury later described the 'very painful scene' in Downing Street, having not seen anyone die before. He also recalled their '30 years' companionship in political life' and reflected 'that now, just before this sudden parting, by some strange misunderstanding which it is hopeless to explain, I had, I believe for the first time in my life, seriously wounded his feelings'. Salisbury then added: 'As I looked upon the dead body stretched before me I felt that politics was a cursed profession.'

# 14

# David Butler's desk, Cambridge

*Thursday, 10 March 1955*

'Cleggy boy, are you in town? Are you around bwoy?' Jeremy Vine is dressed as a cowboy, in jeans, stetson and clutching a gun. He is talking to a computer-generated Nick Clegg, whose commitment to the saloon bar theme extends to a cowhide waistcoat and leather chaps. 'Your leathers might not fit,' Vine says. 'But at least you've got 'em on.' Bizarrely, this tableau, along with taking pot shots at tin cans apparently containing 'Lib Dem Lurve Juice', was designed to explain the vote share Clegg's party had secured in previous elections, and how that might affect the 2008 local election results. Yes, this wasn't even for a general election. This was for 137 district and unitary councils in England and all the councils in Wales.

Whatever David Butler had imagined more than half a century earlier, we can be pretty sure that it was not this. He had something much simpler in mind to explain politics: a pendulum to show the movement in support from one party to another. Doodling at his desk, the swing-o-meter was born. Butler, it is worth stressing, was a nerd. Initially a cricketing nerd, at the outbreak of the Second World War the cancellation of county matches deprived him of new data. So, aged 21, he started crunching the numbers on elections instead. His work on the Cube Rule – which showed that if the ratio of votes between two parties in an election is A:B, then the ratio of seats they will win is $A^3$:$B^3$ – led to a 1950 article for *The Economist*, and even an invitation to brief Winston Churchill on his ideas. (When Churchill, then 75, asked if he was holding his party back, Butler replied, boldly: 'You are not the asset you once were, sir.') Butler shaped and crafted much of what we now consider to be the game of modern politics – he popularised and spread the use of the term 'psephology' to describe the study of elections. For more than half a century he wrote the Nuffield election studies, definitive academic accounts of the campaign and results. He appeared on the BBC's first televised election programme in 1950, at a time when only 2 per cent of the country even had a TV set.

And he pioneered swing: the idea that from one set of results from a constituency or two it was possible to forecast, with some accuracy, the overall general election outcome. So if, say, Labour were up 5 per cent in one result, it was possible to work out how many other seats required a swing of 5 per cent or less for Labour to take them. In early 1955 there was a lot of talk in the BBC about using computing machines to do the number-crunching (and make the broadcast seem more cutting-edge). But it was a lower-tech solution that would change politics forever. In later life Butler would claim that others had created the swing-o-meter, which he then championed. But his biographer, Michael Crick, unearthed letters which prove otherwise.

At home in Cambridge on Thursday, 10 March 1955 Butler sketched out a design for what would become one of the most iconic, and simplest, explainers of the complicated business of elections. In a letter to Grace Wyndham Goldie, a senior BBC producer of election and political coverage, Butler wrote: 'To show people how the tide is going, a simple pendulum might be used. If the pointer is kept at the figure revealed by the electronic calculators as the average swing so far, the total number of seats likely to change will always be available.' He enclosed a pencil drawing of what the pendulum might look like. A couple of months later he wrote again to Goldie, this time calling it a 'speedometer type device'.

In the end the swing-o-meter only made a brief appearance in the coverage of the snap 1955 election, called by Conservative Anthony Eden to gain his own mandate after replacing Churchill as PM. By the 1959 election, though, it was a nine-foot contraption, operated on the night by Butler himself – the only time the inventor would appear with his invention. A young David Dimbleby watched as his father and broadcasting legend Richard grappled with Butler's cutting-edge analysis. 'It was a kind of magic because nobody knew what he was talking about, or how he had discovered this,' says Dimbleby. 'So he was like a sort of magician from the beginning.'

Butler's friend and colleague Bob McKenzie would control the swing-o-meter for six elections from 1964, before the pendulum was passed first to Peter Snow, who swung a heavy metal pointer over an electronic screen which changed colour, and later Vine, whose graphics became increasingly ambitious (and baffling). It didn't always work. In the Dudley West by-election in 1994, the swing from John Major's Tories to Tony Blair's ascendent New Labour was 29 per cent, which Snow's machine could not compute. 'It was too much for it,' Snow recalls. 'The whole screen went sort of blank.' It happened again two decades later in Scotland after the 2015 general election, when a 30 per cent swing to the SNP was too much for the graphics. In fact, Scottish politics helped break the idea of a universal swing across the whole of the UK. In recent years broadcasters have experimented with two, three, even four different swing-o-meters, either to show the regional differences or the interplay between different party combinations. Something in its original simplicity, though, was lost.

'We had enormous fun with the graphics,' says Snow. 'I don't think David Butler was that keen.' On the night of the 2015 election – in which Vine jumped around a virtual Commons chamber and recreated the Lib Dems as a collapsing house of cards – Butler appeared briefly with them on screen. 'I think sometimes we get over-enthused with the graphics,' he said with characteristic understatement.

Vine remembers it well: 'He tried to disguise his feeling of being, I think, quite appalled by the whole snazzery of the graphics. Every time we do a general election now I say, look, let's have the bloody thing made of wood again, as a tribute to David, because in the end that's the joy of it, let's keep it as simple as we can, a piece of wood on a nail.'

# 15

# David Owen's kitchen table, Limehouse

*Sunday, 25 January 1981*

It is a reassuringly British thing that the birth of a new political party be toasted with tea. Like all births, despite being inevitable for months, the moment of truth came suddenly and unexpectedly. With no time to rush to somewhere more suitable, it happened on David Owen's kitchen table. It wasn't that the conception had been an accident, just that all those involved had different ideas about what it might grow into. This was a project with first three, then four parents. The early weeks and months were joyous, surprising, triumphant. Everyone loved each other. But there then followed a messy divorce.

First to the courtship. After James Callaghan lost the 1979 election to Margaret Thatcher, Labour did what parties always do when they lose, and moved even further from the interests and priorities of the public towards the peculiar niche pursuits of the party machine. These hard-left socialists, led by Tony Benn, wanted less private industry, less Europe, less nuclear power. To secure control of the apparatus (an obsession of extreme wings the world over) they wanted the leader to be chosen by unions and members at the annual conference, not by MPs. They also wanted mandatory reselection, allowing sitting MPs to be more easily blocked from standing again.

Michael Foot became leader in November 1980, and the fudge of a plan to create an electoral-college system to choose future leaders and deputy leaders was endorsed at a special conference at Wembley on 24 January 1981. The next day David Owen's wife, Deborah, popped the kettle on at their home in Limehouse, a then-gritty part of east London which had yet to be transformed by the money that would flow into Canary Wharf later in the decade.

Around the kitchen table were the Gang of Four. At 42 Owen was the youngest, and had perhaps most to lose. A neurologist before becoming a Labour MP, he was a defence minister at 36 and foreign secretary at just 38. But he hated the hard-left tendency, who had booed him at the 1980 party conference. Good-looking, smart, charismatic, he seemed destined to one day be prime minister. Instead he chose to leave Labour, and with it any prospect of high office again.

Joining him was fellow Labour MP Bill Rodgers, less well known but an experienced organiser in pursuit of centrist causes, who had been transport secretary in the last Labour government. Alongside was Shirley Williams, then 50, a hugely popular political figure who was a Labour minister in both the Wilson and Callaghan governments and was education secretary when she lost her seat in the 1979 election. Even Tories openly lamented her defeat.

They were the original Gang of Three. The fourth man was Roy Jenkins, who had been both chancellor and home secretary, but left the Labour government in 1977 to become president of the European Commission. As well known for his inability to pronounce his Rs as for his love of good wine, 'Woy' wanted back into British politics and would not entertain Foot's Labour, even if they wanted him.

Despite having just four members, this gang was prone to spats and splits. The Limehouse Declaration might have been the Patshull Road Declaration if a meeting at Rodgers's home in Kentish Town, north London, had not been derailed by Williams and Jenkins arguing about who was going to lead the party that did not yet exist. Rodgers's wife Sylvia was also fed up with providing lunch for them and cups of tea for the reporters outside, so suggested they might meet somewhere else.

So they convened again at Owen's place on 25 January. 'It was an accident really,' Owen says of his kitchen's place in history. 'And one I'm rather proud of but I have no real reason, it was just my turn to have the next meeting.' Journalists were told to gather outside in expectation of an announcement. There would be no rushing those inside. They wrote and rewrote and redrafted and tore up and wrote again the mini-manifesto that would stake their claim to a new politics. In all it went through eighteen drafts.

'Shirley was unhappy about some of the wording,' Owen tells me. 'And then she said, "Oh, I'm on the one o'clock news." So we turned on the one o'clock news around this round table in our kitchen. And there was Shirley being as positive as hell, as she often was. We said, "With what you were saying Shirley, our wording is mild in comparison to what you just said." We laughed and she gave up her reservations. And so we went with it.'

Deborah Owen typed it. 'The calamitous outcome of the Labour Party Wembley conference demands a new start in British politics,' the Limehouse Declaration began. 'A handful of trade union leaders can now dictate the choice of a future Prime Minister. We propose to set up a Council for Social Democracy. Our intention is to rally all those who are committed to the values, principles and policies of social democracy.'

The aims were bold, if a little on the vague side: 'Reverse Britain's economic decline . . . eliminate poverty . . . an open, classless and more equal society . . . a healthy public sector and a healthy private sector . . . a competitive economy with a fair distribution of rewards.'

It was obvious to all involved that this meant a new political party. They just needed a name: having toyed with Democratic Labour, Progressive Labour and even New Labour, by March they settled on what the papers were already calling them: the Social Democratic Party, or SDP. They received 80,000 letters of support in days, 50,000 people became members, and the cash started rolling in, with half a million pounds soon in the bank. So too the defections – twenty-eight Labour MPs jumped ship. In June an alliance was formed with the remnants of the Liberal Party. The voters followed: by December the SDP/Liberal alliance stood at 50 per cent in the polls. Jenkins started to think he might become prime minister. Williams got herself elected in a by-election first, then Jenkins followed. Liberal leader David Steel told his party: 'Go back to your constituencies and prepare for government.' They went back and prepared, and were left disappointed. By the time of the 1983 election the bubble had deflated. The SDP/Liberal alliance got 25 per cent of the vote, and just twenty-three MPs.

Owen has no doubt about what went wrong. 'We got into bed with the Liberals. And as soon as we got into bed with the Liberals, we lost our essential, crucial point to our existence – we were a new party. And gradually that image of us had been eroded with alliances and sharing seats, everything changed. I was ready to fight to build a party. And it was probably going to take ten or fifteen years before it became the government of the country and probably wouldn't have had me as prime minister even by then.'

In the end there were too many ideas about what the point of the exercise had been. Was it to force Labour to see sense with a centre-left programme, and then return to the fold? Was it to be a new centrist party, a mish-mash of the 'best bits' of right and left? Was it to revive the old Liberals of Gladstone? When a formal SDP merger with the Liberals was suggested, Jenkins, Rodgers and Williams backed it but Owen was opposed. When the Liberal Democrats emerged from the wreckage, Owen kept a small rump of the SNP going for a while, with the same flag but without the electoral support. It limped on until 1988. At the final SDP conference in Coventry, Owen made one last leader's speech. Everyone on the platform stood up to applaud, pushed their chairs back, and the stage, the SDP logo and the conference slogan all collapsed. And that was the end of that.

*Municipal*

# 16

# Putney Heath

*Sunday, 27 May 1798*

These days the only shots you'll get on Putney Heath are of the Instagram and espresso variety. But back in 1798 it was the scene of a quite remarkable, and thankfully unrepeated, armed duel. The prime minister of the day, William Pitt the Younger, sixteen years into what would be almost nineteen years in power, went up against George Tierney, the Irish Whig leader of the parliamentary opposition tasked with taking on the government following Charles Fox's secession from the Commons a year earlier. It was a real test of who was quick on the draw.

The row started on Friday, 25 May when Pitt, an oddly colourless politician who somehow still dominated the Tory Party for decades, tried to get the Commons to pass an emergency bill to bolster the Navy in the face of French aggression. There were fears that without it revolution would jump from Paris to London. Tierney insisted he did not oppose the detail of what Pitt suggested, but condemned the 'extraordinary manner' in which the government was trying to bounce MPs into passing the legislation in a single day, warning it would cause public alarm.

Pitt claimed that the 'only motive' Tierney could have to oppose the bill was that of 'impeding the service and defence of the country'. A forerunner of what we might now call 'Why do you hate Britain?', Tierney complained to the Commons Speaker,

Henry Addington, who replied that everyone should wait for the prime minister's explanation. Pitt responded that they would be waiting a long time.

So they took it outside. That night Tierney wrote to Pitt: 'I trust you will recollect what a Gentleman, as wantonly provoked as I have been, has a right to require.' In other words, he challenged him to a duel. Incredibly Pitt accepted, informed the Speaker, and then wrote his will. They were not, it seems, mucking about.

At 3 p.m. on the afternoon of Sunday, 27 May 1798 Pitt arrived on Putney Heath, some six miles south-east of the Palace of Westminster, with his close friend and minister Dudley Ryder as his 'second', or wingman. Tierney was joined by his friend George Walpole, the MP for Derby. It was the day before Pitt's 39th birthday, Tierney was 37.

Ryder and Walpole made some last, desperate attempts to get the whole thing called off, but to no avail. Let battle commence. Cartoons at the time made much of the fact that Tierney was a good deal fatter than the rake-like Pitt, who made for a much less substantial target at which to aim. Pitt and Tierney took their twelve paces. On the count they turned, and pulled their triggers. Both missed. They fired again; this time Pitt gallantly pointed his pistol in the air. And that was that. An official statement released to the press said: 'The Seconds then jointly interfered and insisted that the matter should go no farther, it being their decided opinion that sufficient satisfaction had been given, and that the business was ended with perfect honour to both parties.'

The next day, *The Times* was unimpressed: 'We are sure that the Public at large will think, with us, that a life so valuable as Mr Pitt's, and in which the hopes not only of this Nation, but of every Cabinet in Europe, is concentered, [*sic*] ought not to have been risked to gratify the passions of any man.' William Wilberforce, the God-fearing, Pitt-supporting leader of the movement to abolish slavery, was so incensed about the incident taking place on Whit Sunday that he threatened a motion against duelling, and only backed down a few days later under pressure from the prime minister. Pitt may have emerged unscathed – he wrote to his mother that 'the business concluded without anything unpleasant to either party' – but he came down ill soon after and wasn't seen again in Parliament for the rest of the session, having been told to avoid 'the fatigues of repeated and long debates'.

The incident, though, was the talk of the town. The Court of Common Council, which oversaw the running of the City of London, debated a motion which talked about how freedom of debate was 'the chief pillar and most lasting security' of the privileges enjoyed by parliamentarians and went on to 'seriously lament that the dignity of Parliamentary debate has been violated by terminating in recourse to arms'. Opinion on the council was divided: some of those present wanted to congratulate Pitt for the result of the duel. Others wanted to know why both Pitt and Tierney hadn't been arrested. The motion was withdrawn. However, it cemented the idea that disputes between senior parliamentarians should be decided at the despatch box, not at the business end of a pistol. Even King George III got involved, writing to his prime minister: 'I trust what has happened will never be repeated.'

And it wasn't. At least not between prime minister and leader of the opposition. It would be a full 154 years after Tierney vs Pitt before the leader of the opposition would have a fixed opportunity to challenge his rival during Prime Minister's Questions, which began as fifteen-minute sessions on Tuesday and Thursday afternoons in 1962 under Harold Macmillan, before Tony Blair turned it into a single half-hour in 1997. Now each Wednesday at noon, as the two rivals stand across the despatch box, the one thing of which they can be confident is that the worst that will be fired at them are some tough questions, some overworked soundbites and some lame jokes.

# 17

# St George's Chapel, Windsor

*Saturday, 20 January 1827*

George Canning might have become prime minister sooner were he not so blatant about wanting it. Born in 1770, Canning could be seen as the Boris Johnson of his day: a troubled child packed off to Eton, emerging as a charismatic and funny one-time foreign secretary, prone to dramatic resignations and struggling at times to hide his ambition, even when it might have helped in its fulfilment. He courted the press, too, tearing around the country making speeches in the pursuit of popular appeal. Critics have said of both men that their smart oratory covered up a lack of principle.

Canning, though, came from humbler beginnings than Johnson: his father died when he was one, and his mother, a touring actress, took up with another actor and married him. It was a wealthy uncle who sent young George to Eton, before Oxford, and a brief career as lawyer before setting on his political dreams. In 1792, in a bold example of the maxim 'Don't ask, don't get,' he wrote to the then prime minister William Pitt (the Younger) requesting help in getting a seat in Parliament, and Pitt, amazingly, obliged. Within a few years he was a junior minister for foreign affairs – an area in which he took a keen interest. Canning was a prodigious worker, once declaring: 'The happiness of constant occupation is infinite.'

Then in 1801 Pitt resigned and was replaced by Henry Adding-ton, who Canning did not think was up to much and said so: 'Pitt is to Addington as London is to Paddington.' The jibe meant he was overlooked for higher office. It was six years before he would make the cabinet as the Duke of Portland's foreign sec-retary, but in 1809 Lord Castlereagh, the war minister, discovered that Canning had done a deal with the prime minister to have him sacked. Castlereagh challenged Canning to a duel. Canning had never fired a gun before, and missed. Castlereagh was a better shot, striking his rival in the thigh. Both men resigned in disgrace soon after.

When later Portland stood down, Canning humbly offered himself up to be PM, which George III did not appreciate so went for Spencer Perceval instead, although he only lasted until 1812, when he was assassinated. It's a job to keep up. When Lord Liverpool replaced Perceval as prime minister, Canning had not learnt his lesson and demanded to be both foreign secretary and Leader of the Commons, to stop his old rival Castlereagh holding the latter. Liverpool refused. So it was Castlereagh who would take credit for bringing peace to Europe in 1815 after Napoleon's defeat, before committing suicide in 1822. By now Canning was back as foreign secretary, and when Liverpool had a stroke in February 1827 the king, finally, sent for him in April that year. Unfortunately, the new prime minister was now 56, already ill and getting worse.

On the evening of Saturday, 20 January 1827 the great and the good had gathered at St George's Chapel, Windsor, for the funeral of the Duke of York. It was freezing. And it turned out to be a super-spreader event. The Bishop of Lincoln caught the cold that went round and was dead within less than a fortnight. While the Lord Chancellor was said to have dodged catching it by put-ting his hat under his feet to avoid standing an hour and a half on cold stones, the Duke of Sussex was also suffering and being attended to by doctors. It was soon reported that 'Mr Canning labours under a similar disposition.'

He never fully recovered, and after soldiering on with an inflammation of the lungs, likely pneumonia, he lasted as prime minister for just 119 days before he died on 8 August 1827. Yet his impact on British politics did not end there. John Bew, a professor of history and foreign policy at King's College London who went on to advise Boris Johnson, Liz Truss and Rishi Sunak in Downing Street, has hailed Canning as the 'torchbearer for the "liberal Tory" tradition'. When he became prime minister he split his party, with several Tory Ultras like Robert Peel and the Duke of Wellington refusing to serve under him. Canning, a moderate, reached out to those in the opposition Whigs to join his cabinet, arguably sowing the seeds for the Conservative split and the emergence of the Liberal Party decades later. Though he would never see it.

The newspapers at the time noted that he was the fifth PM to die in office in just twenty-two years. Among those who had passed, Pitt, Fox and Liverpool gained their place in history through their actions and longevity, and Perceval for the manner of his demise, but Canning became reduced, rather unfairly, to a footnote, a punchline and a pub quiz question. His record as the shortest-serving prime minister remained unbroken until Liz Truss's brief stint almost two centuries later. Canning did, though, get a statue in Parliament Square, where he now stands alongside fellow prime ministers Lloyd George, Churchill, Peel, Palmerston, Derby and Disraeli. It might be a while before Truss joins them.

# 18

# Frome memorial hall

*Thursday, 25 April 1929*

'We are not a party created for the production of stunts,' the prime minister told the throng in Frome, without actually being in Frome, which you might argue was quite some stunt. As he geared up for a general election, Stanley Baldwin was in such demand that he could not get to every part of the country, and voters could not be expected to travel to every speech. The speech would have to come to them.

The Conservatives had received so many requests for appearances by their leader that he could agree to barely a quarter. So the party embraced the new technology of the day to relay speeches to other parts of the country. Telephone land wires were specially laid by Post Office engineers, with the Marconiphone Co. providing speakers and amplifiers.

Baldwin had enjoyed popularity in the West Country. During an election tour of the region earlier in 1929 he had been cheered wherever he went and was even showered with flowers at Taunton. So he chose to repay the compliment with his most audacious broadcast yet: becoming the first person to address eight different audiences simultaneously by giving a single speech in Bristol.

Early in the evening Baldwin arrived in Bristol, dining at the Grand Hotel in Broad Street before making the short journey through the city centre to Colston Hall. (Opened nearly 150 years after the death of the slave trader Edward Colston, the concert hall was renamed the Bristol Beacon in 2020). That night in 1929 large queues had formed outside before the doors opened at 7 p.m., with newspaper reports highlighting how women made up a 'large percentage' of the crowd. As the 5,000 punters filed in they were encouraged to buy small Union Jacks, which they waved while an organist led the crowd in singing 'Land of Hope and Glory' and 'It's A Long Way to Tipperary'.

Meanwhile at Frome memorial hall, a boxy building opened four years earlier as a tribute to those killed in the First World War, the crowds arrived early too. They spent an hour singing, led by local noted conductor Mr Bennett, with Mr Young on piano. When Geoffrey Peto, the Conservative MP for Frome, arrived they burst into 'For He's a Jolly Good Fellow'. He was cheered onto the stage. But nobody was here to see him. They had not come to see anything, it was what they had come to hear broadcast all the way from Bristol.

At 8 p.m. a film was shown of Baldwin's travels around the country, meeting and greeting and shaking hands. Exactly the sort of thing that even today plagues the start of every leader's party conference speech. Then, at 8.10 p.m., the switch was thrown and Frome went live to Bristol, the words of the prime minister travelling twenty-five miles down the specially laid Marconiphone landlines. During the speech a picture of Baldwin was projected onto the screen. 'The whole meeting was beautifully timed, and the broadcast was quite audible,' the *Somerset Standard* reported, approvingly.

The same scene was being played right across Somerset. At the same time thousands were gathering at the Drill Hall in Shepton Mallet, the Drill Hall in Bath, Bridgwater town hall and venues in Yeovil, Weston-super-Mare and flower-wielding Taunton. Some 10,000 gathered in Colston Avenue, just outside the venue where Baldwin spoke, to hear the speech relayed by the local newspaper, the *Bristol Times and Mirror*. A mile and a half away a further 20,000 people were at an open-air meeting on Bristol's Durdham Downs.

Baldwin was an unassuming, private man who paradoxically was capable of engendering great loyalty among his supporters. In his speech he hit back at his critics, who said he was unable to rouse an audience to its feet, saying such exhibitionism was 'the last thing I want to do.' He railed against the socialism of Labour's Ramsay MacDonald and tried to make a virtue of under-promising, mocking the back-to-work plans set out by Lloyd George as a 'corpse reviver for the Liberal Party'. Baldwin boasted that the 'evil' of unemployment had dropped by a quarter of a million in two months, and trade was improving. 'It is vital that nothing should occur at the present time to disturb that upward movement.'

Like so many politicians who fear they are on the way out, he also lamented the constant clamour for the new: 'The appetite which seeks for a fresh sensation in politics, if not every day, at least on Sunday, is a depraved appetite.' Those behind today's Sunday newspapers and political TV programmes should perhaps take note. Baldwin went on to quote Edmund Burke: 'Our first duty is not to be popular, but to run straight.' He succeeded on the first part. After five years in office he called the election for 30 May, and Labour emerged as the largest party. Baldwin's Conservatives lost a staggering 152 MPs, including Geoffrey Peto in Frome.

# 19

# Chard guildhall

*Saturday, 9 May 1992*

Not many famous people come from Somerset. Aside from The Wurzels, obviously. When I was growing up, Paddy Ashdown was a local legend. He was not even our MP down on the Somerset Levels, but the Liberal Democrat leader's national reputation as a swashbuckling, straight-talking, square-jawed, squint-eyed Marine who swapped MI6 for politics was a source of pride beyond his Yeovil constituency and spread across the whole of the South West.

In the run-up to the April 1992 general election it seemed to many as if he might actually end up in government, with much talk of a Labour minority administration requiring Lib Dem support. It came to nothing. John Major won a surprise victory for the Conservatives. And that was the end of that. Or at least it would have been, had Ashdown not been such a relentless force of nature. To supporters he was a tireless campaigner, to critics a tedious self-publicist, but either way it was just what the third party needed.

'Leaders have two reactions to general elections,' recalls Alan Leaman, who was Ashdown's speechwriter and adviser. 'One is they collapse and go away for a bit. Or they try to set the agenda for the next phase of politics, even though they are completely exhausted and a bit disappointed about the result.' Ashdown chose the latter course of action. 'Looking back, it was extraordinary. Having dealt with all he had been through, it would have been easy for Paddy to say, "I am going to have a rest".'

'All he had been through' included the revelation in February 1992 that five years earlier Ashdown had a five-month affair with his secretary Tricia Howard, captured in the *Sun* headline 'Paddy Pantsdown', which Ashdown himself described as 'Dreadful – but brilliant.' It did not do him much harm, his personal ratings rose after the scandal broke, and the Lib Dems held all but two of their seats in the 1992 election. No disaster, then, but far from the breakthrough Ashdown craved. In the wake of the result Neil Kinnock had resigned, triggering a Labour leadership contest between Bryan Gould and John Smith. While that battle was being played out, Ashdown decided to insert himself into the debate.

One hopes it is not indelicate to point out that it has been a while since governing alone has been a realistic prospect for the Liberals. So the question of what they might do in a hung parliament had long been a problem. During the Liberal/SDP Alliance years and the 1987 election campaign, David Steel and David Owen could not agree on what to do about the two bigger parties. Owen was keener to work with Thatcher than was Steel, who wanted a Labour government.

Ashdown became leader of the new Liberal Democrat party born out of the Liberal/SDP merger in 1988, having promised to replace Labour as a party of the left. When that did not work, in large part because Labour bounced back under Kinnock, Ashdown adopted a policy of a plague on both their houses, declaring in 1991: 'Is Labour better than the Tories? Or are the Tories better than Labour? The answer is simple. They're just as bad as each other!'

This position of 'equidistance' lasted through the 1992 general election campaign, but caused major headaches when Lib Dems were pressed on whether they would really prop up Major if he lost his majority, after thirteen years of Tory rule. So Ashdown resolved, in the immediate aftermath of the election result, to change that – to make it explicitly clear that the Lib Dems favoured working with Labour to remove the Tories.

A Big Speech was in order. It had to be carefully drafted, walking the tightrope between being too radical so as to startle the horses, or too cautious and the horses not noticing at all. Leaman wrote a draft, Ashdown scribbled on it, Leaman incorporated some (though not all) of the leader's changes. And then the process was repeated many times over. Ashdown shared it with prominent journalists, including Andreas Whittam Smith of *The Independent*, to gauge reaction and interest. Party strategists met for hours in the days before the speech, trying to get the balance right.

The preparation worked. On the morning of the speech on Saturday, 9 May it was one of the top stories on Radio 4's *Today* programme, with Charles Kennedy, then party president, sent out to the airwaves to explain the shift. Several newspapers previewed it. Ashdown called Leaman and asked him to make contact with Tony Blair, then shadow employment secretary but identified as a rising star. 'Can you get hold of Tony and explain what we are doing?' When Leaman called he got Cherie Blair instead, who abruptly insisted Tony was busy in his Sedgefield constituency.

The speech was to be delivered in Chard, a small market town in Ashdown's constituency where he was already due to hold a meeting. That Saturday lunchtime coincided with the FA Cup, with Liverpool and Sunderland fans making the long journey to Wembley. At the same time, around forty or fifty Lib Dem supporters made the journey from across Devon, Dorset and Somerset to Chard guildhall, though they were not the intended audience for the speech. Which is why Ashdown spent far more time checking the TV cameras to make sure the shot of him on stage was just right than worrying about his colleagues.

The Guildhall itself is a striking two-storey building of the local pale-yellow hamstone, its impressive two tiers of columns and domed clock tower dominating the main road through the market town. In the speech he warned of 'almost permanent one-party Conservative government', and claimed that 'Labour can no longer win on their own.' He went on to stress that he wanted 'a ferment of ideas, not the clicking of calculators' working out 'mathematically constructed pacts and alliances'. Instead he wanted 'to work with others to assemble the ideas around which a non-socialist alternative to the Conservatives can be constructed, with Liberal Democrats at the centre of the process and a reformed voting system as the starting point'. He added: 'We must be much less exclusive in our approach to politics than we were in the last Parliament, and much more inclusive to others in this one.'

It landed well on the day. That night Ashdown drank a bottle of Irancy rosé with his wife while watching the coverage on the BBC and ITV News. 'They said that my proposals had split Labour,' he wrote in his diary. 'Couldn't be better!' But by Monday morning many Lib Dems were up in arms. One MP, Liz Lynne, told Ashdown she would lead a revolt against him in what he later described as the worst conversation he had ever had with a parliamentary colleague. Doors were slammed. As the days and weeks passed, things got worse. In one meeting Ashdown desperately likened himself to Columbus setting off to discover India but finding America instead – he and his shipmates would discover nothing, he argued, if the good ship Lib Dem stayed in port. Lib Dems who believed their supporters were soft Tories voting to keep Labour out feared for their seats as a result of the madcap idea. Veteran Lib Dem MP Russell Johnston punningly dismissed the Chard speech as a 'burnt offering'. By mid-June things were so bad that a special hotline had to be set up so cross party members could record their anger on tape. Eventually Ashdown prevailed: the party finally abandoned equidistance at its annual conference in 1995. He was back in control, yet so much of what followed was outside his grasp: John Smith's death, the Tory collapse, Tony Blair's incredible rise.

That New Labour went on to secure a landslide victory with 418 seats can give rise to the assumption that the Chard approach failed. All that talk of Ashdown sitting at the cabinet table came to nothing. Yet in the 1997 election the number of Lib Dem MPs more than doubled to 46, the highest for a third party since 1929. The Ashdown effect in his own backyard was huge, winning seats not just in Somerset but in Devon, Cornwall and Avon. Across the South West the Lib Dems actually outpolled Labour by 31 per cent to 27 per cent, winning 14 seats, just one fewer than Labour. The Lib Dem vote share in the region was almost double the 17 per cent secured across Britain. The prevailing mood of 'Get the Tories out' meant that in many of those seats voting Lib Dem was the only option. Closer alignment with Labour, as advocated in Chard, had worked.

Ironically it was only when the Lib Dems readopted equidistance that they finally got into power. In the 2010 election Nick Clegg was careful as the party's leader not to commit to either party, clearing the way for coalition talks with the Tories and Labour, and five years in power with David Cameron's Conservatives. Five years later, when the Lib Dems fought an election apparently in bed with the Tories, the exit poll predicted they would lose 47 of their 57 seats. On live TV Ashdown said: 'If this exit poll is right, I will publicly eat my hat on your programme . . . I will get one specially for the occasion.' In fact the exit poll was wrong: they actually lost 49, including Ashdown's old seat, which meant even Chard turned blue.

# 20

# Tennants auction house, Leyburn

*Saturday, 18 October 2014*

Even just in the car park it is clear to any onlooker that there is money here. Then from the smart driveway up to the imposing yellow-stone façade, which opens up to the sweeping twin white marble staircases of its dramatic pillared entrance hall, Tennants auction house is designed to impress. This is where the discerning people of North Yorkshire come to be dazzled by the bling on display, but they want to know exactly what it is they are buying. Just two years earlier the family-run auction house had broken the million-pound mark for a single lot, selling a Chinese blue and white porcelain vase for £2.6 million.

On a Saturday in October 2014 the punters were not queuing up for Old Masters, fine jewellery or polished antiques. They were here to choose an MP. And not just any MP. Not some provincial workhorse who would cut the ribbons and keep the constituency happy. No, they had become used to having a local representative of national, even international, distinction.

William Hague was standing down as MP for Richmond in North Yorkshire after a quarter of a century, which had included serving in the government of John Major, four years as Conservative leader up against Tony Blair in his pomp, and then returning as David Cameron's respected foreign secretary. His predecessor as Richmond MP was Leon Brittan, who spent twenty years in Margaret Thatcher's government, as home secretary and trade secretary, before quitting the Commons to become vice-president of the European Commission. His predecessor was Sir Timothy Kitson, who served as parliamentary private secretary to prime minister Edward Heath from 1970 to 1974. His predecessor was Sir Thomas Dugdale, a former Conservative Party chairman who was a whip in Neville Chamberlain's war government, and then minister of agriculture in Winston Churchill's last government. You get the idea. This was a true-blue seat, had voted Conservative for more than a century, and the party members believed they were picking a future member of the cabinet, not merely a member of Parliament.

When Hague announced in July 2014 that he would quit the Commons at the next election, his seat – with its ultra-safe majority of 23,336 – was eyed up by some of the party's most promising names. In all, around 350 people applied. Nick Timothy and Stephen Parkinson, both aides to Theresa May during her time as home secretary and later prime minister, threw their hat into the ring. They made it onto the nine-strong long list, but were eliminated during interviews at the Golden Lion, a traditional hotel in Northallerton, where candidates shifted uneasily in red-leather armchairs before making their way across thick, heavily patterned carpets to face their inquisitors.

The four who went through to the final selection at Tennants were: Wendy Morton, the local girl who had been a pupil just up the road at The Wensleydale School, and had been a doughty chairman of the Richmond Conservative Association until she stepped down to apply for the seat; Chris Brannigan, a former lieutenant-colonel in the Royal Scots Dragoon Guards who had served on eleven operational tours and was working as manager of the Weiss Gallery, so would have known his way around Tennants' artworks; Robert Light, a local councillor, serving as leader of the Conservative group on Kirklees council, where he had once been council leader; and then there was this chap called Rishi Sunak, who had barely set an expensively shod foot in Yorkshire before the process started and came with a CV stuffed with references to Oxford, Harvard and Goldman Sachs.

Yet by the time the four rivals were making small talk over the vast Yorkshire spread laid on backstage at Tennants, Sunak was inching ahead as the favourite. He had impressed in early rounds, and with plenty of money already in the bank he was also able to commit to the job of getting selected full-time, unlike his rivals.

More than 300 people from across the constituency packed into the main hall. 'This was like being brought out as the prize lot at an auction,' recalls Brannigan. 'You took a peek through the gap in the curtain at the size of the audience and thought "bugger me" what sort of crowd is this?'

The crowd included, on the front row to the right of the stage, the piercing eyes of Hague, Brittan and Kitson. Just behind them sat Field Marshal The Lord Inge, a former chief of the defence staff and proud Richmond resident. This was a long way from a handful of party stalwarts in a draughty village hall who usually pick a candidate over a Thermos of tea. 'This was the Las Vegas of selections,' Brannigan adds. 'It really did feel like you were going on sale.'

The MP for neighbouring Skipton and Ripon, Julian Smith, was the auctioneer/chair of the event. He was very strict. Lots were drawn, with Morton going first, followed by Brannigan, Sunak and then Light. Each candidate would get two minutes to make their pitch, with Smith cutting off anyone who went even a second over. Then it was opened out to a relentless barrage of questions about foreign affairs, the economy, and the really tricky: 'What do you have in common with a farmer?'

Sunak had faced mutterings about his suitability for country life. His slight frame had led some locals to joke about how he could ever join a day's shoot: 'He doesn't look like he could hold a double-barrelled shotgun.' Even as they arrived, some of the members were still insisting to Hague that 'what we need is a good York-shiremen like you, or it's got to be a farmer, or somebody local'.

When the votes were counted, Sunak romped home on the first ballot, beating the military man, the local councillor and the local party bigwig. He had won over not just the three grandees on the front row, but most of the rest of the room too. Morton was visibly upset. It is hard not to feel some sympathy. She had done everything on paper that a candidate might be expected to do. All that knocking on doors, stuffing envelopes, early-morning canvassing, late-night meetings. If anything, she was too local. Whether it was national political ambition or parochial snobbishness, the local Conservative members did not want the Wensleydale lass. She was not part of the ruling country squire set who still dominated in these parts. Having taken the result pretty badly, Morton left Tennants as quickly as she could.

Also struggling to come to terms with the result was Akshata Murty, Sunak's wife of five years, who was comforted by others at the thought of moving from London to North Yorkshire. Give it a bit of time, she was told. And they did. They threw themselves into country life. Sunak bought himself some blue wellies, which marked him out as a townie to proper rural, green-booted locals. He won them round, though, with pre-dawn visits to dairy farms to help out with milking and learn about the industry by getting his hands dirty.

Race was an issue, albeit not a defining one. As a British-Asian man chosen to represent an area that was 95.3 per cent white, it was depressingly inevitable. Sunak took to retelling a story about how he was introduced early on to a Yorkshire farmer as 'the New William Hague'. The response: 'Ah yes Haguey! Good bloke. I like him. Bit pale, though. This one's got a nice tan.' It did not matter. Sunak won the seat comfortably in 2015, and by the 2019 election, when he was chancellor in Boris Johnson's government, his majority of 27,210 was bigger even than anything Hague secured. And the Richmond grandees got what they wanted in October 2019 when their man became prime minister.

What is extraordinary about this story is that Morton played a part in her rival's rise to the top. She had picked herself up, dusted herself down and in 2015 got elected as Conservative MP for Aldridge-Brownhills (a seat where local boy Nick Timothy also lost out again). When Liz Truss became prime minister in September 2022, among her many eyebrow-raising decisions was to promote Morton, then a middle-ranking railways minister, to the role of chief whip. Far from first choice, she found herself in charge of discipline (and HR) among Tory MPs. But she struggled to command the respect of her colleagues, who unkindly nicknamed her Wendolene, her helmet of auburn hair and rictus grin bearing a passing resemblance to the love interest in *Wallace and Gromit*. There were even reports that Truss had tried to ban her chief whip from meetings, telling aides: 'I just don't want to have her in here. I just hate her.' Truss denies saying this.

Even so, on 18 October 2022, exactly eight years to the day since she lost to Sunak for the Richmond selection, Morton took the chief whip's seat near the window at the far end of the cabinet table, while Sunak was licking his wounds on the back benches. In the wake of the disastrous mini-Budget and sacking of chancellor Kwasi Kwarteng, Truss was clinging on by her fingertips. Half of Tory Party members wanted her to quit. The PM's official spokesman boasted that she had got through the cabinet meeting without anyone calling for her resignation. A triumph.

The next day Suella Braverman was forced to resign as home secretary after leaking sensitive papers to her supporters. The Labour Party had also tabled an opposition day debate and vote on fracking, keen to embarrass Tory MPs into voting for Truss's unpopular policy of resuming drilling for shale gas. Conservative MPs were told that it amounted to a confidence vote in the government so must vote it down. Then a minister said that it was not a confidence vote; others said it was. There were reports of backbenchers being manhandled into the right voting lobby.

In the confusion Craig Whittaker, Morton's deputy chief whip, was seen marching around declaring: 'I am fucking furious and I don't give a fuck any more.' He was said to have resigned. Morton was also reported to have quit because Number 10 had undermined her position. Then Downing Street insisted they were both in post. Jacob Rees-Mogg went on Sky News to clear things up, but admitted that he was 'not entirely clear' whether Morton had quit. It didn't matter.

It was one debacle too many. The Truss experiment was over. She resigned the next day, complaining that 'given the situation, I cannot deliver the mandate on which I was elected by the Conservative Party'. She was gone within five days, and with her went her chief whip Morton, who watched on TV as her old rival Sunak, the man who outbid her at Tennants auction house, finally took the lot.

# 21

# Windmill Street, Gravesend

*Thursday, 19 March 2015*

Tom Hanks's alarm goes off at 5 a.m. Tom Hanks sits up in bed in blue pyjamas. Tom Hanks says: 'I really wanna stop but I just got a taste for it.' Tom Hanks checks the bags under his eyes in the bathroom mirror. Tom Hanks drinks water. Now Tom Hanks is walking down a street, pointing and waving and high-fiving and fist-bumping in brown leather gloves. Tom Hanks signs an autograph, is given a table tennis bat and hits a ping pong ball out of shot. Tom Hanks poses for selfies, hails a taxi, makes calls and reads texts. Tom Hanks watches as a bright-yellow car drives past in slow motion. Tom Hanks dances in the street.

Now imagine all of that, but instead of Tom Hanks it's Nick Clegg. And instead of the streets of Manhattan, it's the streets of Gravesend on an overcast day in March 2015. The Lib Dems were facing electoral wipeout after five years in coalition with the Conservatives. Having tried everything to turn the party's fortunes around, a plan was hatched for Clegg to star in a shot-for-shot recreation of the music video for 'I Really Like You' by the Canadian singer Carly Rae Jepsen, which originally starred Hanks walking the streets and lip-synching. The homage was the brainchild of James Holt, the party's deputy director of communications, who hoped Clegg would go viral and voters would see he could at least laugh at himself. Clegg said he did not 'want it to be too po-faced and serious'. But when he got on set, he was as bemused as the passers-by in Kent who watched as the actual deputy prime minister waved at a yellow Mini, took selfies and walked past three women swiping right on his Tinder profile.

That Thursday in March was supposed to have been a big day for the Lib Dems: Danny Alexander, the chief secretary to the Treasury, was due to unveil his own Lib Dem Budget to draw a distinction between their policies and George Osborne's Tory austerity. He even posed outside the Treasury with a bright-yellow Budget box, which made him look less like a chancellor and more like Beaker from *The Muppets* had got a new lunchbox. In the Commons hardly anyone turned up to listen to Alexander's statement, and Clegg was seen leaving halfway through. Thick with a head cold and running a temperature, Clegg was not rushing off to attend to important matters of state, but to get into a car for the thirty-mile drive to Gravesend. After a busy day pretending to be Tom Hanks pretending to be Carly Rae Jepsen, Clegg got back into his car and thought to himself: 'Why the fuck did I do that?' It is a question that, even now, nobody is quite able to answer.

Election expenses filed by the Lib Dems show that the music video was made by north London-based Create Productions, which boasted on its website: 'Our passion is production and we know how important it is to produce new, fresh and exciting video content working to your budget and timelines.' The invoice billed the party for work to 'film and edit parody of Carly Rae Jepsen video', costing £7,800 after VAT. A parody of 'Uptown Funk', the number-one single by Mark Ronson and Bruno Mars, was also planned, with the lyrics rewritten to promote Lib Dem policy. This, sadly, was never made. Both videos were attempts to recreate the 'success' of Clegg's filmed apology for ditching opposition to tuition fees, which was later remixed by The Poke website as a song, becoming an internet hit and reaching 143 in the UK singles chart.

You might be wondering how you had forgotten that the Clegg/Hanks video existed. Well, despite costing the best part of £8,000 and a day of the deputy PM's time, it was never released. Holt later reflected that he was lucky to have 'had colleagues that stopped me from making it public'. Maybe keeping it secret was a mistake. Only seven weeks after the video was made, the Lib Dems slumped from 57 MPs to just 8. Clegg hung on before finally making his escape (well, he was released by the voters of Sheffield, Hallam) in 2017.

Since then he has gone on to get a proper job at Facebook parent company Meta, becoming 'president of global affairs' (which is a job title that Boris Johnson has long been competing for). And yet still Clegg won't release the tape. Just how bad is it? Given the muck that can be found online these days, there is clearly something especially egregious if even the bloke at Facebook thinks it shouldn't be online. In July 2021 I launched a petition to get the video released. It got 303 signatures. With that level of support, I now know how Clegg felt on election night in 2015.

# 22

# Car park, Hastings

*Saturday, 2 May 2015*

There is a scene at the beginning of Stanley Kubrick's *2001: A Space Odyssey* where the monkeys (or at least actors dressed as monkeys) wake up and find something has landed in their patch of dusty rock, apparently from space. They screech and leap around, against a soundtrack of eerie soprano warbling, nervously creeping closer to the huge black rectangular slab which is sticking out of the ground. The sun rises over the top edge of the monolith, marking the dawn of mankind, as suddenly the apes acquire the intelligence to use rocks and bones as tools, initially to break things and then to club each other to death. One suspects this was not what the Labour Party's biggest brains had in mind when they decided to carve their 2015 election pledges onto a similar stone tablet. But when news of this idea spread among party staff a week before polling day, a mixture of disbelief, fear and dismay prompted several of them to share clips of the Kubrick movie.

In the end it was Labour officials themselves who set about trying to club each other to death over the stunt, the fallout of which almost a decade later remains so raw that, remarkably, none of those closest to it will speak on the record even now. 'It's still quite painful,' one of those involved tells me. Another says: 'It has genuinely been too difficult a subject for people to discuss even together in darkened rooms for years.' A third key figure also demurred from an on-the-record conversation: 'I haven't got much interest in getting into it I'm afraid.' A fourth said: 'I can't. I just can't.'

In the final fortnight before the 2015 election, the polls suggested that the Conservatives and Labour were neck and neck. The big event in the campaign calendar had been Ed Miliband's decision to do an interview with piratical poseur Russell Brand, who had previously told his fans not to bother voting at all. During their fifteen-minute YouTube exchange in Brand's kitchen, the comedian-turned-conspiracy theorist complained about 'unelected powerful elites', and Miliband insisted 'It's not about being edgy.' This meeting of minds is what Labour spinners had been worried would be the reason why the 2015 campaign would be remembered. They were wrong.

By this point Miliband was exhausted, drained by eighteen-hour days criss-crossing the country with his closest aides, including Bob Roberts, the director of communications, just doing as they were told by HQ. The campaign was being coordinated from a war room set up in a side office at 1 Brewer's Green, Labour's glass-and-steel three-storey headquarters. At the heart of this team were Spencer Livermore, the campaign director, Paddy Hennessy, the deputy director of communications, Lucy Powell, a Labour MP and vice-chair of the campaign, and Torsten Bell, the head of policy.

Together they closely guarded the famous 'grid', the hour-by-hour matrix of announcements, briefings, visits, media appearances and stunts which Miliband and his team would embark on in the final days of the campaign. Paranoia in the war room was so widespread that the blinds on the windows had been closed to prevent the Tories from spying on them from neighbouring buildings. Had David Cameron got his binoculars out and managed to sneak a peek at the Labour grid he might have been baffled by one entry for Saturday, 2 May 2015, which said simply 'Quarry Event'. It was no less perplexing to some of the most senior figures in the Labour campaign. Having been otherwise engaged in the day-to-day of a campaign already into its fifth week, it was only on Thursday, 30 April that concerns started being raised about what exactly the 'Quarry Event' involved. 'What the fuck is that?' asked one official, who had belatedly clocked it on the grid.

It was, it transpired, the brainchild of Bell, the wonkish former Treasury adviser who helped write the party's manifesto. Colleagues were told enigmatically that Bell, a keen rock climber, had 'connections with someone in the quarrying business'. The original idea was to have Labour's key election pledges carved into a rock face. When that proved unfeasible, it had been decided that they would instead be etched onto a stone slab. 'You are just taking the piss,' said one official after being told belatedly of the plan. 'Go away, I've got work to do, don't do this to me. It's not true.' But it was. And it was too late to stop it.

On Sunday, 3 May *The Observer* carried a low-key 300-word story on the bottom-right-hand corner of page three. The article began: 'Ed Miliband has commissioned a giant stone inscription bearing Labour's six election pledges that is set to be installed in the Downing Street Rose Garden if he becomes prime minister. The 8ft 6in-high limestone structure is intended to underline his commitment to keep his promises by having them literally "carved in stone" and visible from the offices inside No 10.' The decision to brief this stone-cold scoop to one friendly paper meant that already-sceptical rivals had even more reason not to take it entirely seriously. By this point, the 'limestone structure' – which would soon become known as the 'EdStone' – was already out there. It had been photographed, under embargo, for the benefit of waiting cameras the day before in an overcast car park by the sea.

On the morning of Saturday, 2 May Miliband was in the car on the way to Hastings when photos were sent through of what he was going to be unveiling. Although he had been vaguely aware of a stone-based stunt on the grid, this was the first time he had actually seen it. 'Bob, Bob, doesn't it look a bit like a gravestone?,' the Labour leader asked his top spin doctor. 'Fuck off Ed, we'll put some balloons around it,' Roberts replied. The pair then discussed turning round and cancelling the photo op. But in previous days they had vetoed at least three other 'gimmicky, silly' ideas from campaign headquarters, and feared a revolt if they withdrew from this one at such a late stage. With some trepidation, they pulled into the car park of Hastings Academy and clapped eyes on the thing for the first time. And Ed was right, it looked a lot like a gravestone.

'I want the British people to remember these pledges, to remind us of these pledges, to insist on these pledges,' Miliband told a crowd up to one deep in places. They were not waving Bob's promised balloons but small pink flags, huddled around blue scaffolding which was supporting the limestone lump. (An early plan to unveil it in a school had been dropped over concerns that the floor might collapse under the weight.) To add to the comic scene, in the background could be seen a trailer bearing an election poster for the Green Party and, for some reason, a tethered horse. The carved pledges on the stone themselves lacked in excitement what they also lacked in specificity: 'A strong economic foundation. Higher living standards for working families. An NHS with the time to care. Controls on immigration. A country where the next generation can do better than the last.'

Nobody can quite explain how or why it happened. Stewart Wood, then a Miliband adviser, once told me: 'My involvement was standing at the side of it in Hastings watching it get unveiled, with the guy who sculpted it standing next to me saying, "Don't you think it's a good bit of work?" and me saying "It's . . . you know . . . a great bit of sculpture."' It was the work of Basingstoke firm stoneCIRCLE. The firm's boss, Jeff Vanhinsbergh, later helpfully admitted to being a Tory voter, joking: "It does seem that stone was the final nail in the coffin for Ed Miliband."'

On Monday, 4 May the picture of the event appeared prominently on the front of *The Guardian* and *Financial Times*, with smaller inserts on page one of *The Sun* ('Off his rock-er') and *The Daily Telegraph*, but much of Fleet Street was more distracted by the recent birth of Princess Charlotte. On the inside pages it was perhaps one of the first examples of papers running 'internet memes' as political news, showcasing how Miliband had been mocked up variously as Moses, Mount Rushmore and Christ the Redeemer. The funereal undertones were hard to ignore, appearing to be a gravestone to a recently deceased political party. The Conservatives leapt on it too, David Cameron saying he had thought it was a joke and 'had to check first it wasn't April 1 because I just couldn't believe this was a serious proposition' and Boris Johnson called it 'some weird commie slab' and 'the heaviest suicide note in history'. Simon Blackwell, the comedy writer, declared the whole thing beyond parody: 'Ed Miliband builds a policy cenotaph. And you wonder why we stopped doing *The Thick of It?*'

More problematic was that the great slab cast a shadow over the detailed plans for Labour's final days of campaigning, including carefully planted stories revealing a £2 billion deficit in the NHS and a leaked recording of John Major, the former Conservative prime minister, admitting to a 'pretty substantial underclass' in poor areas across the country despite five years of the Tories being in power. It fell to Lucy Powell, a regular media firefighter, to face more mockery of the masonry. She didn't really help matters when she went on BBC Radio 5 Live and said: 'I don't think anyone's suggesting the fact that he's carved them into stone means that he is absolutely not going to break them or anything like that.'

By this point the piss-taking was relentless, and continued until polling day, when the Conservatives shocked even themselves when they won a majority of 12 seats. Amber Rudd, the Conservative MP for Hastings and Rye where the unveiling took place, publicly thanked the EdStone for its role in holding her marginal seat. Nobody seriously thinks it was the EdStone that cost Miliband the election in the final days – polling inquests later confirmed that they had overestimated Labour support throughout the campaign and the Tories were likely always ahead. The near-total collapse of the Lib Dems – down from 57 seats to just 8 – had also been unexpected, and unquestionably helped the Tories.

However, the image of the EdStone, like the bacon sandwich photograph where Miliband made a meal of his breakfast, perfectly illustrated what the public already suspected about his

unsuitability to be prime minister. 'It definitely reinforced nega-
tives that people already felt about Ed,' says one former aide.
'There were bigger factors at play, but this was an image that captured them all together.' It became a physical monument to the
dysfunctionality of a party which was not ready for power. If that
is what they come up with in opposition, a voter might have been
forgiven for thinking, what would they do with the nuclear codes
and the keys to the Treasury? Jon Snow, the *Channel 4 News*
anchor, performed his own on-air eulogy: 'Labour hoped it
would be a hinge stone, many thought it was a henge stone, it was
quickly tagged an #EdStone, but now it's just a headstone.'

The blame game was brutal. Damian McBride, the former
Brown spin doctor and henchman, knew who was at fault, tweeting: 'For those who don't know Torsten Bell, the #Edstone architect, he's one of those arrogant oafs with brains to spare but no
common sense.' Months later Bell told the BBC: 'Lots of ideas in
the heat of politics come and go. We did a big service to British
journalism by providing that level of fun and amusement for a
considerable period.' Pressed on the whereabouts of his brainchild, he replied: 'I can't tell you where the EdStone is but I can
tell you that we will not be going into stonemasonry any time in
the next few years.'

After Labour's defeat a nationwide search was launched for the
stone. *The Sun* set up a hotline, while the *Daily Mail* offered champagne to anyone with information regarding its whereabouts. The
People's History Museum in Manchester made a plea to add it to
its collection. A version appeared at The Ivy Chelsea Garden restaurant, but this appears to have been a fake. Indeed, Labour
insiders insist that it was destroyed soon after polling day. As was
Miliband's leadership – he resigned within hours. Even that was
not the end of the saga. In October 2016 Labour was fined a
record £20,000 by the Electoral Commission for undeclared 2015
election spending, including the £7,614 spent on the EdStone.
Making it one of the most expensive electoral suicide notes, as
well as the heaviest. Maybe some balloons would have helped.

# High days and holidays

# 23

# European Museum, St James's

*Monday, 11 May 1812*

If the paintings had been marginally more engrossing, the prime minister might have lived. Anyone hooked in by the gallery hype would have thought it impossible for the 'nobility and gentry who patronise and admire the fine arts' or indeed anyone else to drag themselves away from the masterpieces for any purpose, never mind an assassination.

John Wilson, a brash American art dealer from Charleston in South Carolina, had opened his European Museum on King Street in St James's almost a quarter of a century earlier. He offered a 'safe and eligible' market to those seeking to dispose of their collections, and to the discernible buyer he promised the greatest variety of original pictures to 'gratify his taste and enrich his cabinet'.

But anyone could go and have a look. Subscribers could get an annual pass for them and a friend for a guinea, or you could just turn up on the day and pay a shilling. Which is almost certainly what John Bellingham did when he arrived at the museum at around 2 p.m., on a day out with his landlady Rebecca Roberts and her son. They spent a couple of hours touring the show-rooms, where more than 400 paintings, sculptures, ceramics and curiosities were on display, awaiting new buyers.

The blockbuster attraction that day was a depiction of the entombment of Christ by the Italian painter Leonello Spada, a seventeenth-century follower and imitator of Caravaggio. Just the day before, *The Observer* had predicted there would be 'one constant scene of bustle and astonishment, as all the world naturally press forward to have a peep at that wonderful picture' before it was shipped off to Russia. That morning Wilson had taken out a prominent advert on the front of *The Morning Chronicle* in which he described *The Miraculous Entombment* as 'the most astonishing effort of art in the universe'.

However astonishing it might have been, Bellingham might have been forgiven for not having his mind fully on the Baroque brushstrokes. What with the two guns he was carrying. One nine-inch steel pistol was hidden in the secret left-hand pocket he had a tailor sew into his dark-brown coat a fortnight earlier. Another was stuffed into his thick nankeen yellow pantaloons. With his yellow and black striped waistcoat, made of toilinet woven from wool and silk, and his stout hessian boots he would have looked quite the fashionable gentleman in his early forties. He was also, oddly, carrying a pair of opera glasses. When you're already packing two guns, why not add something else to your pockets?

Bellingham, it seems fair to say, was not a mentally stable man. He was an impoverished businessman who had been arrested in 1804 in Archangel, Russia, over unpaid debts when a venture there went wrong. He spent his five years in prison blaming the British government for a lack of assistance, before returning to England and taking up his grievance in person. Instead of settling down quietly with his wife and family at home in Liverpool, he took lodgings at 9, New Millman Street in London. Clearly desperate, and increasingly so, he petitioned the Foreign Office, the Treasury, the Privy Council, Number 10, every MP and even the Prince Regent, complaining of being 'bandied about from man to man, and from place to place'. Someone at the Treasury told him to stop making further applications to the government 'and that I was at full liberty to take such measures as I thought proper for redress'. So he decided to shoot the prime minister, Spencer Perceval. In taking such measures, Bellingham's odd logic went, he would get his day in court to publicly make his case for government compensation for his business woes.

Perceval was a 49-year-old father of twelve, and had been prime minister for two and a half years. Were it not for the manner of his leaving office, his premiership might have been entirely forgotten. Even as the only British prime minister to be assassinated, his place in history is most likely as a Trivial Pursuit answer rather than that afforded to the iconic US presidential murders. Perceval is more Garfield and McKinley than Lincoln and Kennedy. Unlike most of his contemporaries, the prime minister did not drink, gamble or hunt. Noted as a strong, if solid, leader, he was a staunch opponent of Catholic emancipation and slavery – the latter of which has given rise to conspiracy theories about whether his killing was a plot orchestrated by Liverpool traders angered by legislation abolishing the Atlantic slave trade and controversial government Orders in Council which created a naval blockade around Napoleon's France. He was also deeply unpopular with the Luddites, who took to smashing up looms in protest at the pace of technology taking their jobs. Despite the idea of a shadowy network at play – as put forward by Andro Linklater in his highly seductive if low-evidence book *Why Spencer Perceval Had to Die* – Bellingham always insisted that he acted alone that May day in 1812.

After spending a couple of hours admiring the best the European Museum had to offer, it was a little after four o'clock when Bellingham and his guests emerged again on to King Street. Roberts and her son went home to New Millman Street, with Bellingham saying something about needing to go to Westminster to buy a prayer book. In fact, during weeks of reconnaissance, he had got to know the layout of the Palace of Westminster and the comings and goings of Parliament.

That afternoon Perceval was due to appear in Parliament for the start of hearings into the Orders in Council at 4.30 p.m., so would have been expected to pass through the lobby a few minutes before. Bellingham was too far away, picking up his pace as he fought his way through the crowds on Whitehall.

Helpfully, Perceval was also running late and had not left Downing Street. In fact, by the time he arrived at Parliament just after 5 p.m. his assassin was waiting, catching his breath, in the corner of the lobby. Unlike most people in Britain at that time, Bellingham knew exactly what the prime minister looked like, having spent weeks staking out the Commons, dining in the coffee room and watching proceedings. Security was almost non-existent, compared to today's ring-of-steel fortress, and members of the public could come and go as they pleased.

As soon as the target came through the door, the gunman stepped towards him. His right hand reached into the secret pocket and pulled out the small pistol, pressed it against Perceval's chest, and pulled the trigger. The lead musket ball entered the left side of his chest, pulverising his heart. Blood spread across his white waistcoat. 'Murder!' the prime minister exclaimed as he fell. The dying prime minister was rushed on to a table in the Speaker's apartments, but within twelve minutes he was dead.

Bellingham had the pistol taken from his hand, and then calmly walked over to a bench and sat down. Guards locked the doors, but there was no need. Far from making an attempt to escape, he waited for his arrest. Asked if he was the man who killed the prime minister, he replied: 'I am the unhappy man.' He was led to the bar of the House of Commons, identified as the assassin, and had the second gun taken off him. After being questioned in a committee room, he was committed to trial and a hackney coach was called to take him to Newgate. But an anti-government crowd had begun to gather, and some cheered the killer and tried to help him to escape. Instead Bellingham was smuggled out of the Speaker's entrance.

On Tuesday, 12 May Bellingham woke from a good night's sleep in jail, had a breakfast of tea and bread rolls, then wrote a note to Roberts, his landlady, describing how his mind was 'tranquil' for the first time in eight years and asking for her to send him 'three or four shirts, some cravats, handkerchiefs, night-caps, stockings . . . together with comb, soap, toothbrush, with any other trifle that presents itself which you think I may have occasion for, and enclose them in my leather trunk'.

That afternoon the Commons sat only for tributes to the slain prime minister, Speaker Abbott writing in his diary: 'In most faces there was an agony of tears; and neither Lord Castlereagh, Ponsonby, Whitbread, nor Canning could give a dry utterance to their sentiments.'

Whatever was packed in his trunk, Bellingham was still wearing the same chocolate-brown coat and striped waistcoat when he went on trial at the Old Bailey on Friday, 15 May. In a lengthy statement to the court in defence, Bellingham said that he had 'no alternative but to sink into utter ruin, or to take the melancholy step' of shooting the prime minister. 'I was incited,' he added,' by the hope of bringing into Court my unfortunate case . . . I trust that this serious lesson will operate as a warning to all future ministers, and that they will henceforth do the thing that is right, for if the upper ranks of society are permitted to act wrong with impunity, the inferior ramifications will soon become wholly corrupted.' He concluded: 'Gentlemen, my life is in your hands . . . I know not what your verdict may be, but sooner than suffer what I have done for the last eight years, five hundred deaths would be preferable. If I am destined to sacrifice my life, I shall meet my doom with conscious tranquillity.' And he did. The whole trial lasted barely eight hours. It took the jury less than a quarter of an hour to reach a guilty verdict.

It was a wet morning on Monday, 18 May when a small crowd gathered for Bellingham's execution. Still wearing the same dark coat and striped waistcoat, he asked the executioner to tighten the rope on his arms so that he would not struggle. Witnesses saw him wipe away a tear before climbing the scaffold almost with a spring in his step. Some in the crowd cheered him, others called for silence. Asked if there was any last communication he wished to make, he started talking about Russia again before being told to stop. He thanked God for having enabled him to meet his fate with 'so much fortitude'. As the clock struck eight, that fate was met, less than a week after he had set off from home with his landlady and her son to look at some paintings.

Perhaps as he had stared at *The Miraculous Entombment*, with three men and two women gathering around Christ's body in mourning, Bellingham might have wondered how his target might be mourned too. In fact Perceval has been largely forgotten, along with the story of the only British prime minister to be assassinated. The site of the European Museum is still home to priceless artworks, having passed to James Christie and become Christie's auction house in 1823. Just around the corner, behind an anonymous-looking door, is a staircase leading up to a smart suite occupied by David Cameron, a prime minister who had to find a new base after his time in office came to an abrupt end. Which was at least something that Perceval did not have to worry about.

# 24

# Midland Hotel, Birmingham

*Saturday, 20 April 1968*

Nothing has changed. Yet everything has changed. The Victorian grandeur of the staircase. The marble pillars. The stained glass. The leatherbound books. The tourists and business travellers milling about. Half a century on, Enoch Powell would still recognise the old Midland Hotel as the place where he ended his frontline career, and with it the idea that there was a place for overt racism on the front bench of either side of the Commons.

Yet there is also much about the place he would not understand, or appreciate. The man who railed against the madness of allowing hundreds of thousands of black people to come to Britain would surely be appalled that on the day I visit what is now called the Burlington Hotel, in the heart of his native city, there is not one member of staff who is white. Powell 0, modern Birmingham 1.

Cocktail of the day in the Berlioz Bar is the not very British, but quite delicious tequila sunrise. The widescreen TV 'hidden' in a gold picture frame is a little *déclassé*. It takes a while to work it out, but I realise that emerging quietly from the bar's hi-fi is a recognisable tune in an unusual setting: It's Britney Spears's 'Toxic' being played on what sounds like a sitar. More of a Wagner fan, Powell would have hated it. On that, if little else, he would have been right.

On Saturday, 20 April 1968, the shadow defence secretary and MP for nearby Wolverhampton South West addressed one of the Midland Hotel's crowded meeting rooms as it hosted the West Midlands Area Conservative Political Centre. In doing so, he smashed the fragile political consensus on race. It came days before Harold Wilson's Labour government was to introduce the 1968 Race Relations Bill into the Commons. Edward Heath's Conservatives had belatedly decided to vote against, to the anger of younger, liberal Tories.

'The supreme function of statesmanship,' said Powell, clutching his papers against his three-piece suit, his receding dark hair slicked back, 'is to provide against preventable evils.' One such evil, he suggested, was the growing 'immigrant and immigrant-descended population'. He called for a reduction in immigration numbers to 'negligible proportions' and urged a policy of urgent repatriation. He claimed that not all immigrants wanted to integrate in Britain; instead they sought to foster racial and religious differences 'with a view to the exercise of actual domination, first over fellow-immigrants and then over the rest of the population'.

And he added: 'As I look ahead, I am filled with foreboding. Like the Roman, I seem to see "the River Tiber foaming with much blood".' He never actually used the phrase 'rivers of blood', but it became shorthand for his quoting of Virgil's epic poem *The Aeneid*. (Strictly speaking, while Virgil was a Roman poet, the character who spoke of the bloody Tiber was actually a Greek prophet, but classical inaccuracy was obviously not the main problem with the speech.)

Powell focused especially on the Windrush generation of 'Commonwealth immigrants and their descendants', most of whom were from the Caribbean, and black. He predicted that by the year 2000 there would be 'five to seven million' of them in Britain. This looking ahead three decades to forecast descendants of descendants was an exercise in panic, not maths. In reality, by 2000 there were around 3 million people in the UK who were born outside the European Union, compared to about a million from inside the EU. Two decades later again, the numbers in the UK born in the EU had trebled to 3 million, while non-EU had only doubled to 6 million.

With guttural emphasis, almost spitting the words, he went on: 'We must be mad, literally mad, as a nation to be permitting the annual inflow of some 50,000 dependants . . . It is like watching a nation busily engaged in heaping up its own funeral pyre.' In an address packed with characteristically sharp imagery, and sharper turns of phrase, he claimed that Labour's planned Race Relations Bill, which would ban discrimination in housing, employment and public services, was like 'throwing a match onto gunpowder'.

Like any savvy politician trying to make a contentious point, he recalled a conversation with an unnamed constituent who had helpfully, and eloquently, said: 'In this country in fifteen or twenty years' time the black man will have the whip hand over the white man.' There was also an elaborate tale of a woman in Wolverhampton who was now the only white person in a street taken over by 'Negroes', who was abused by her black neighbours, and 'finds excreta pushed through her letter box'. Powell went on: 'When she goes to the shops, she is followed by children, charming, wide-grinning piccaninnies. They cannot speak English, but one word they know. "Racialist," they chant.' Did they, though? In the days after the speech journalists tried to trace the woman, but she could not be found and it is still disputed decades later.

*The Times* called it an 'evil speech', and noted that it came barely a fortnight after the assassination of Martin Luther King Jr in Tennessee. *The Guardian* said it was a 'shame' for frontline politics to lose a man of Powell's 'strength and intelligence', but said neither of the main parties 'can afford to give office to men who appeal to be fanning the flames of racialism'. The

*Sunday Mirror* called him 'the erudite Alf Garnett of the Tory party'. The speech, which lasted forty-five minutes, ended with applause, and within barely thirty-six hours ended Powell's career in frontline politics.

Saturdays are normally where news, and political speeches, go to die: no daily journalists to cover them, Sunday hacks too caught up in their own exclusives to worry about live events. Powell, though, knew exactly what he was doing. He briefed his words to some journalists as early as Friday afternoon, cutting out the role of Conservative Central Office in approving and distributing frontbenchers' speeches. He also invited in a TV camera. 'I'm going to make a speech at the weekend,' he told a friend, journalist Clement Jones of the *Express & Star.* 'And it's going to go up "fizz" like a rocket; but whereas all rockets fall to the earth, this one is going to stay up.' Powell himself came back to earth with a bump.

Unlike the local paper, Edward Heath, the Conservative leader of the opposition, knew nothing about Powell's speech until it landed in the Sunday papers. After a lot of very Heathite dithering, at 9 p.m. on Sunday, 21 April the Tory leader telephoned Powell and fired him as defence spokesman in the shadow cabinet, saying the speech had been 'racialist in tone and liable to exacerbate racial tensions'. Heath went on to talk about the need for immigration to be 'most stringently limited', something most subsequent Conservative leaders have promised over the years.

Yet in 1960s Britain, Powell was no extreme outlier. He received 120,000 letters of support. The day after his speech 700 members of the nearby North Wolverhampton Working Men's Club voted unanimously in favour of a 'total ban on coloured people', amid predictions by some that Powell would have the safest seat in Britain. A group of east London dockers and Smithfield porters marched on Parliament chanting, 'We love Enoch Powell'. Fifty steelworkers in Wolverhampton went on strike for half a day in protest at the sacking. York University

Conservative Association said Powell would be very welcome in their city. A Tory MP insisted that the speech chimed with the public mood, telling *The Guardian* at the time: 'You could call him Mr National Opinion Powell.'

It is true that Powell's popularity with much of the public soared. He was re-elected as a Conservative MP until 1974, when he suddenly quit the party to become a Ulster Unionist Party MP in South Down, remaining in the Commons until 1987. Yet the change ushered in by his most famous speech was that never again would a frontline, mainstream politician be permitted to be so blatantly racist – even if, as polls suggested at the time, large majorities of the public agreed with what he had said. Dog whistles hinting at race have not gone away, but Powell drew a line in the sand which front-bench politicians must not cross without losing their job. Instead 'Enoch was right' became a slogan of the National Front, the forerunner of the British National Party.

Nigel Farage, the on-off Ukip leader, spoke often of his admiration for Powell and actually tried, unsuccessfully, to get him to stand for his party. He too complained of parts of the country becoming 'unrecognisable', but as a result of European migration. The key difference is that these migrants were, mostly, white. At the 2014 Ukip spring conference Farage committed the conversational sin of describing in detail a recent train journey, which is only marginally better than the criminal act of talking about your dreams. 'It wasn't until after we got past Grove Park that I could actually hear English being audibly spoken in the carriage. Does that make me feel slightly awkward? Yes.' He later clarified: 'I'm not saying people on trains should be forced to speak English,' although as anyone knows the most English thing is not to speak on trains at all.

The 'Rivers of Blood' speech did huge, long-term harm to the Tories too. In 2013, Sajid Javid, who went from being the son of a Pakistani bus driver to the cabinet table, said the damage done by Powell was something the Tories 'still haven't been able to shake off' almost half a century later. They don't help themselves. In 2007 Nigel Hastilow, a former editor of *The Birmingham Post*, was forced to quit as a Tory candidate in the West Midlands after writing a column declaring 'Enoch was right'. Fifteen years later, George McAleese resigned as deputy chairman of Gosport Conservative Association after sharing a picture of Powell on Facebook with the message: 'Every single day this man is proven more right.' What's odd about this is that nobody under the age of 50 would even recognise the moustachioed dandy in a three-piece suit and pocket square. Told it was 'Powell', they might well think it was the chap who started the Scouts.

One of the most striking aspects of Powell's legacy is that the descendants of the Commonwealth immigrants he railed against not only prospered, but went on to join and indeed lead the party he represented. It is perhaps the greatest rebuff to Powell that the Conservative's top ranks have included Rishi Sunak, James Cleverly and Priti Patel, who had grandparents and parents who arrived from Africa in Britain in the 1950s and 1960s. When Cleverly was challenged by the *Sydney Morning Herald* in 2022 over whether Britain had confronted its colonial past, he replied: 'You're asking the black foreign secretary of the United Kingdom of Great Britain? Yeah, I think the answer is yes – you're looking at it, you're talking to it.'

'I may have failed,' Powell said in an interview twenty years after his infamous speech. 'That does not mean I was wrong.' Yet he was. The number of migrants and their descendants he feared was actually much higher. Nobody would claim that the path of integration has been smooth, and Britain remains a country still grappling with evidence of institutional racism which leaves non-white people treated as second-class citizens, but nor have we seen the rivers, or anywhere else, foaming with blood as Powell foretold.

Even decades after that speech in a Birmingham hotel on a Saturday afternoon, Powell remains synonymous with a strain of racist politics against which the mainstream parties must, rightly, still define themselves today. As Britney would have told him if the sitar allowed, 'Don't you know that you're toxic?'

## 25

# Penmaenuchaf Hall Hotel, Snowdonia

*Thursday, 6 April 2017*

Theresa May is not one of life's conversationalists. Which is odd because politics is essentially hours and hours of small talk occasionally punctuated by someone stepping away briefly to actually do something. In the summer of 2017 I was at a drinks reception at Number 10 where she worked her way around the garden making the opposite of relaxed, easy chitchat. Usually at these things a 'donut' of journalists forms around the host prime minister, with people craning their necks to catch a prime ministerial *bon mot*. With May, guests would spin off like a Catherine wheel to escape being trapped in a conversational quagmire. On this occasion, and with it being the summer, someone asked about holidays. When are you going on your holidays? Where are you going on your holidays? How do you relax on your holidays? What will you be reading on your sunlounger on your holidays? And she replied (I swear I'm not making this up): 'I like books.' Quite the raconteur.

It might have been better if she had done more reading and less thinking on her previous holiday earlier that year. Packing her bags for Snowdonia in early April, May was riding high in the polls. Really high. The latest YouGov survey had the

Conservatives on 42 per cent, while Jeremy Corbyn's Labour Party was on 25 per cent. That was landslide territory. As she and husband Philip checked into Penmaenuchaf Hall Hotel, at the foot of Cadair Idris, the highest peak in southern Snowdonia, she knew it was Labour who had a mountain to climb. She was considering a snap general election.

Not that the Mays didn't get to enjoy the sort of holiday you might expect of a couple in their late fifties (albeit with a couple of security guards in tow). They embarked on a two-and-a-half-mile hike in the hills and woods surrounding Dolgellau, following a £4.95 guide by local author Michael Burnett. The writer later told *The Guardian*: 'During the walk there are a series of revelations. Those moments of discovery are mind-cleansing. They focus you, give you that moment of clarity you need to make those important decisions.' May agreed. 'Walking in Wales is an opportunity to get out and about and see scenery and clear your mind and your thinking,' our favourite anecdotist told *Wales Online*. 'We stay in a hotel and try to walk every day. Walking is about relaxing, getting exercise and fresh air.'

The Mays also went to church, and visited an arts and crafts shop in Dolgellau, where she was sold a Celtic ring made by Barmouth jeweller Anna Hicks and some Welsh slate coasters from Matt Fletcher of Set in Stone. And she was sold on the idea of going to the country. 'Before Easter, I spent a few days walking in Wales with my husband, thought about this long and hard and came to the decision that to provide that stability and certainty for the future, this was the way to do it – to have an election,' she later told ITV News. 'I trust the British people. The British people gave the government a job to do in terms of coming out of the European Union and I'm going to be asking the British people to put their trust in me in ensuring we deliver a success of that.'

The British people declined. During a disastrous campaign, which included tearing up a flagship policy on social care while insisting 'nothing has changed', the Conservative poll lead collapsed. Having inherited a working majority of 17 from David Cameron, far from increasing her mandate she lost it. On 8 June the Conservatives went down 13 seats, with Labour gaining 30. A hung parliament. It was a disaster, and left May reliant on the right-wing, Leave-supporting DUP to pass anything in the Commons. Brexit reached a stalemate.

As ever in politics, success has many fathers, but failure is an orphan. Nobody wanted to take credit, or more accurately blame, for what had happened. While the final decision had been taken up a mountain, the idea of a snap election had been discussed in the foothills for months. As May became keener on the prospect, Nick Timothy and Fiona Hill, her chiefs of staff, had brought in Stephen Gilbert, who ran Cameron's successful, majority-winning campaign, who in turn brought in Lynton Crosby, the so-called Wizard of Oz, who had masterminded election victories in both Britain and Australia. On Thursday, 16 February May called them all to Chequers for a secret summit to discuss the election she had publicly ruled out numerous times. Chris Wilkins, May's speechwriter, gave a presentation on how to make her the candidate of 'relentless change'. Crosby, who had carried out polling which showed strong opposition to an election, dismissed Wilkins's pitch as 'classic populist woolly bullshit'. The talks went on and on.

When they broke for lunch, the guests were served chicken lasagna and boiled potatoes. Mmm, chicken lasagna and boiled potatoes. Bland, stodgy and unimaginative, Theresa May called the general election anyway.

# 26

# Pyramid Stage, Glastonbury

*Saturday, 24 June 2017*

It's quite something when you first stride out in front of the Pyramid Stage crowd at Glastonbury. It is easy to let all the attention go to your head. It is important to know that they are not there for you. The pretty girls with daisies in their hair and sunburnt boys in bucket hats (and your old French teacher) only want you for your ice-cream.

At least they did the year I made my rite-of-passage pilgrimage to Pilton, parking my vintage stop-me-and-buy-one bike – a large freezer mounted on a tricycle – slap bang in the middle of the Pyramid field. A summer job scooping around Somerset had culminated in not just free entry but being paid to work at the greatest show on earth. That June weekend in 2000 I basked in glorious sunshine, the air thick with the doobie and rumours about how many people (including, it transpired, my old French teacher) had scaled, demolished or otherwise overcome the fence. I was being paid to watch Cypress Hill, Reef, Semisonic, Brand New Heavies, Jools Holland, Burt Bacharach and, late on Sunday, with the ice-cream bike packed away, David Bowie. That is who the crowds were here for. Not me and my range of artisan flavours.

Seventeen years later, Jeremy Corbyn did not learn this lesson. Tens of thousands of people flooded into the Pyramid field for a victory rally for the man who had lost. On 8 June he had deprived Theresa May of a majority in the general election (though she would remain as prime minister for another two years). A fortnight later, just after 4 o'clock on a warm Saturday afternoon, sandwiched between rapper Craig David and hip-hop duo Run The Jewels, Corbyn took to the stage of the festival born of the same alternative, hippie, pro-CND politics of the early 1970s which was, and remained, his lodestar. Michael Eavis, the founder of Glastonbury and another bearded old leftie, introduced his friend as the 'hero of the hour'. The crowd, as big as that for some of the world's biggest music stars, roared.

It had been a tough couple of years for the politics of Glastonbury. In 2016, the result of the Brexit referendum had come through in the early hours of the first day of the festival, putting a dampener on the Remain-dominated crowd that no downpour could ever achieve. Then a year later the crowds gathered again in the wake of a political defeat, but this time behaving like winners.

In white trousers and a blue linen shirt, Corbyn took the mic and, like so many to have graced that stage, belted out his greatest hits. "Everyone we meet is unique, everyone we meet knows something we don't know,' he said. They cheered. 'In every child there is a poem, a painting, music.' More cheers. 'Politics is actually about everyday life. It's about all of us: what we dream, what we want, what we achieve and what we want for everybody else.' They cheered yet again, perhaps suggesting they would cheer whatever gobbledegook he came out with.

He quoted one of his favourite poets 'who wrote many, many poems', Percy Bysshe Shelley: 'Rise like Lions after slumber / In unvanquishable number – / Shake your chains to earth like dew / Which in sleep had fallen on you – / Ye are many – they are few.' More cheers, the like of which a nineteenth-century Romantic poet could only dream. 'Racism is wrong, evil and divisive in our society,' Corbyn said. They cheered even louder. Nobody thought about the small issue of anti-Semitism in Labour. All that was yet to come.

Instead they waved placards declaring 'JC HOPE' and 'Jezz you're the one'. Many wore T-shirts with his face on. Chants of 'Oh Jeremy Corbyn!', to the tune of The White Stripes' 'Seven Nation Army' rang out for hours as the crowds dispersed, pumped up by his passionate, if rambling, peroration: 'Let us be together and recognise another world is possible, if we come together to understand that, understand the power we've got, and achieve that decent, better society where everybody matters and those poverty stricken people are enriched in their lives and the rest of us are made secure by their enrichment, thank you very much Glastonbury, thank you inviting me here today, I'm proud to be here, thank you very much Glastonbury.'

Giddy as he walked off the stage, Corbyn fancied he could get used to that rock-star reception. So too his closest aides and family. Tommy Corbyn, the Labour leader's son, later recalled: 'Afterwards one of the Glastonbury staff tapped me on the shoulder and said, "You know he just got a bigger crowd than Rihanna."' In fact Rihanna had never played Glastonbury, but these were mere details.

The seeds had been sown for a plan to harness the power of the Pyramid Stage for Labour's own political gain. After six months of bathing in the Glasto glow Ian Lavery, the Party chairman, had a big idea. He announced to colleagues in December 2017 that he wanted to organise something 'full of energy, that's exciting, and big'. Labour Live was born.

It would bring together all of Corbyn's big-name supporters for a one-off concert in June 2018, raising money for the party's election war chest and hammering home the message that all the cool kids voted Labour. One official told Gabriel Pogrund and Patrick Maguire in *Left Out*, their account of the Corbyn chaos: 'In 2017, we had so many celebrities endorsing Jeremy – I think people just thought that would translate into them wanting to perform for free.'

Socialists always think everything should be free. The music artists, and their management, had other ideas. Ed Sheeran quickly declined. Stormzy was high on the target list. Someone even sent the grime rapper a contract confirming his Labour Live appearance. It was remembered by Labour staff for two reasons: first, it bafflingly used three different fonts, and second, and perhaps more importantly, Stormzy wasn't available to appear. They had booked White Hart Lane recreation ground in Tottenham and set the date – 16 June – without confirming that any acts were free and willing. Courtney Pine, the jazz musician, had been 'confirmed' by Team Corbyn, though this came as a surprise to the saxophonist's management, who 'confirmed' that not only was he not playing, he wasn't in the country. Even Labour stalwart Billy Bragg had other plans. Marsha-Jane Thompson, the Corbyn aide tasked with making Labour Live a success, became hung up on the idea of booking 1980s Brummie reggae outfit UB40, until a younger colleague snapped in a meeting: 'Fucking let UB40 go! Nobody fucking likes UB40!' In the end they could only dream of a band as high-profile and successful as UB40.

The biggest musical act on the bill ended up being The Magic Numbers, an indie band who enjoyed their most notable success while New Labour was in power and hadn't since troubled the charts for a decade. Music bible *NME*, which had been briefly enthusiastic about Corbyn a year earlier, took one look at the billing and declared it 'a missed opportunity, and one that's about as cool as Corbyn's shell suits'.

Initially charging £35 a pop, for weeks the party had struggled to sell even a tenth of the 20,000 capacity. Through discounts and giveaways they crawled to 'sales' of around 13,000. There were reports that the festival's drinks supplier was refusing to bring kegs of beer because there would not be enough people to empty a barrel.

Tickets sales were so poor that the Unite union had to step in and buy 1,000 of them to give away. In an attempt to shovel tickets out of the door, anyone could claim the freebies. One person booked twenty-three tickets in the name of Kim Il-Sung, while

*Guardian* journalist John Crace received 'eighteen in the name of Tony Blair c/o HMP Belmarsh'. MPs were urged to pose with 'Labour Live props' for social media pictures. After twenty-four hours just three had complied: one of them got the web address wrong and another admitted he would be 400 miles away in his Lanarkshire constituency on the big day.

It was so pathetic that days before the event even Theresa May, not a woman known for her comic timing, ripped into Corbyn about it at PMQs: 'I have heard that the right honourable gentleman is trying to organise a music festival, Labour Live. I will pass over the fact that it is going to have a "solidarity tent", which obviously won't have any Labour MPs in it. I do not know if all members of the House are aware of the headline act at Labour Live. The headline act at Labour Live are the shadow chancellor and The Magic Numbers – that just about sums them up.'

On the day they just about got away with it. The line-up fell some way short of the Glastonbury vibe they were emulating, featuring as it did Sex Pistols bassist Glen Matlock, winner of *The Voice* Jermain Jackman and Reverend and The Makers, whose chart success was only marginally more current than The Magic Numbers. One name on the bill more notable now than then was Sam Fender, who in June 2018 was virtually unknown but within eighteen months would have a number-one album.

The problems with the low-profile line-up continued on the day. 'So loved Clean Bandit set at #Labourlive,' tweeted front-bencher Barry Gardiner. 'Couldn't resist asking them for a selfie afterwards.' The eagle-eyed spotted that not only was it not a selfie (someone else took the picture), but whoever the people he was standing with were, they were not 'Rockabye' hitmakers Clean Bandit. Unlike at Glastonbury there was no one with a stop-me-and-buy-one bike, but Unite union boss Len McCluskey had an ice-cream van which played 'The Red Flag' instead of 'Greensleeves'.

On the main stage there was a rendition of 'All You Need Is Love' before John McDonnell, the shadow chancellor, came on to introduce his old friend: 'I had a dream we'd have a socialist in Number 10 and it'll be this socialist, Jeremy Corbyn!' In his twenty-five-minute set, Corbyn reprised much of the material from Glastonbury a year earlier. 'I look in the House of Commons, across the aisle, at a party of the rich, by the rich, for the rich and funded by the rich and I see a party over there that's divided, incapable of negotiating and incapable of governing.' But Magic Grandpa had, by now, lost some of his lustre. Twelve months of wrangling over Brexit had caused deep divisions in his own party too.

On the eve of Labour Live ninety Labour MPs defied their leader's instruction to abstain on a Commons vote to keep Britain in the single market. On the day of the event, midway through Corbyn's speech, pro-EU campaigners unfurled a banner calling on him to 'stop backing Brexit'. That summer Labour were still neck and neck with the Tories in the polls. Two and a half years – and a change of prime minister – later, in the December 2019 election Corbyn led Labour to its worst defeat in eighty-four years.

If Glastonbury 2017 was the height of the cult of Corbyn, then Labour Live marked a new low. And it came at a cost. 'No, Labour Live did not make a profit,' Diana Holland, the party treasurer, admitted later that year. 'I don't think that was why it was organised, however, there was a net cost. It'll be included in next year's financial report.' Except it wasn't. Any mention of Labour Live in the accounts presented to the 2019 party conference was gone. And within months Corbyn would be too.

# 27

# Barnard Castle

*Sunday, 12 April 2020*

There are two opticians in Barnard Castle on the day I visit the town: Specsavers and Bayfields. Unless you also count the eye-test chart hanging on the wall of The Stables Café, where the town's name is spelt out in decreasing-sized letters. It is an inside, albeit well-worn, joke about a town which didn't ask to become the focus of the nation's ophthalmological mirth.

Barney, as it is known by the locals, is the sort of smart market town you get far more often in the North than those in the South realise: well-known chains cheek by jowl with independent cafés, Christian bookshops, charity shops, butchers, bakers and if not candlestick makers then plenty of candle sellers in the sort of boutiquey interiors shops which sell 'Live, laugh, love' coasters and exist solely for panicked dads to drag children into for last-minute Mother's Day gifts.

Dominic Cummings was panicking the day he arrived on the outskirts of town, but for different reasons. As the prime minister's closest adviser, he had abandoned Downing Street for his family home in Durham on Friday, 27 March 2020, at the height of lockdown restrictions. His journalist wife, Mary Wakefield, had come down with Covid. The couple worried about what to do if they both got ill and nobody could look after their child – a fear felt by millions of other parents across the country that spring. Unlike those worried millions, the Cummings clan travelled hundreds of miles to his father's remote farm, where his two young nieces could look after their son if needed. After a couple of weeks there Cummings had recovered from his own bout of Covid. Unsure if he was well enough to embark safely on the long drive back to London, he did what anyone would do and um . . . went for a drive.

As he later explained to an incredulous nation on 25 May at a press conference in the Downing Street garden: 'My wife was very worried, particularly given my eyesight seemed to have been affected by the disease. She didn't want to risk a nearly 300-mile drive with our child, given how ill I had been. We agreed that we should go for a short drive to see if I could drive safely.' Makes sense – test your eyesight by driving a car. With your wife and child with you. Safety first.

'We drove for roughly half an hour and ended up on the outskirts of Barnard Castle town.' That's quite a long eye test. 'We did not visit the castle.' No point. Had he climbed the steps up to the castle's scruffy grey-blue gates he would have found them chained shut. What with there being a pandemic on. 'We did not walk around the town.' Shame, it's very pretty. 'We parked by a river.' The River Tees is a broad, roiling torrent, crashing over rocks as it passes through Barney, ultimately connecting the Pennines with the North Sea. Climbing out of the car, you get a blast of fresh air, cooled by the water below. Maybe that helped Cummings feel a bit better. 'I felt a bit sick.' Or maybe not. 'We walked about ten to fifteen metres from the car to the river bank nearby. We sat there for about fifteen minutes.' How nice. On your wife's forty-fifth birthday too. 'We had no interactions with anybody.' Thank goodness for that, what with there being a pandemic on. 'An elderly gentleman walking nearby appeared to recognise me. My wife wished him Happy Easter from a distance, but we had no other interaction.' Ah, so some interactions?

On and on he went. So much detail, which only served to provoke more questions than it answered. Like so many big political scandals, what stuck in the mind was not the dates and times, the ins and outs of who got ill when, who went where, when, or why. What was striking was this supposed Whitehall brainbox, the great political strategist of our age, claiming that he got behind the wheel of his car to test his eyesight. That is self-evidently funny, and he appeared to be laughing at those who had done the right thing, stayed at home, not travelled the length of the country to be nearer relatives. Of course none of it would have come out were it not for the drip-drip reporting of both the *Daily Mirror* and *The Guardian*, which pieced together eyewitness accounts of Cummings out and about when being out and about was banned. That Downing Street repeatedly denied it, and that Wakefield wrote about this period for *The Spectator* without mentioning the trip north, made the final public admission all the more damaging.

There is also much of his story which does not add up. The drive from London to County Durham is long. Really long. The idea that a couple in their forties and a 4-year-old son could make the 275-mile, five-hour journey without stopping suggests bladder control unknown to mere humans like you or me. Cummings the clairvoyant also claimed in his press conference that 'only last year I wrote explicitly about the danger of corona-viruses', except it turned out that a March 2019 blogpost had been edited to insert the reference to coronavirus and Chinese labs on 14 April 2020 – the day after he returned from Durham.

There was also the question of the reason for the gallivanting. The story appeared to change when Cummings gave evidence in May 2021 to a parliamentary inquiry into coronavirus. He claimed that the escape to the country actually wasn't about childcare after all, but because his home had been the target of a 'gang of people outside saying that they were going to break into the house and kill everybody inside'. It had been decided, he claimed, that he would move his family out long before they got sick. In an interview a few weeks later with the BBC's Laura Kuenssberg he again claimed that there was more to it than just his family's sickness, that in the Rose Garden he 'didn't go into all the details for various reasons', and that he 'had repeated security problems at my house going back to 2019'.

Except he did go into all of this in the Rose Garden in May 2020; he explicitly mentioned security as mitigation: 'I was subject to threats of violence. People came to my house shouting threats. There were posts on social media, encouraging attacks. There were many media reports on TV showing pictures of my house . . . I thought the best thing to do in all the circumstances was to drive to an isolated cottage on my father's farm.' He included that excuse at the time, but the public did not buy it then either. It is also not entirely clear why these threats were not something that should be dealt with by the police, rather than a mad road trip which broke the rules he had helped draw up.

The bizarre Rose Garden press conference had an immediate effect on both Boris Johnson's popularity and public faith in the government's Covid strategy. Some 59 per cent thought Cummings should leave Number 10 (something he wouldn't actually do for another six months, when Johnson sacked him in a wild power struggle involving his chief adviser, spin doctor and wife). Between April and June 2020 the proportion of people who said Johnson was doing well as PM fell from 66 per cent to 43 per cent, according to YouGov. The proportion who thought the government was handling the coronavirus well dropped by similar levels.

'The whole thing was a complete disaster,' Cummings said later. 'It undermined public confidence in the whole thing.' He suggested that if he and Johnson had come clean, the public would have understood. This is, arguably, doubtful. 'We both made a terrible Horlicks of it in a very odd circumstance,' he added. On that, at least, we can agree. The strange tale of the Barnard Castle eye test was all true, though. 'If I was going to make up a story,' Cummings told MPs, 'I'd have come up with a hell of a lot better story than that one, right? It's such a weird story.'

Indeed it is. And it is one that inspired a weird tourism boom too – English Heritage reported that in 2021 the site of the eleventh-century fortress which once belonged to Richard III had enjoyed its best-ever year for visitors, up 20 per cent on 2019. That is a lot of people walking around making eye-test jokes. But without them I would not have spent a pleasant day in Barnard Castle, nor would I have found myself in The Stables Café, marking that historic day Cummings was seen in town by ordering the most appropriate item on the menu: Spotted Dick.

*Water*

# 28

# Peasholm Park lake, Scarborough

*Wednesday, 6 April, 1842*

What do David Cameron, Peter Mandelson, Gerry Adams, Anthony Eden, Boris Johnson and Robert Kilroy-Silk all have in common? For a brief time they were the Lord of the Manor, albeit a manor at the bottom of a lake in Scarborough. It was, though, the only way to escape parliament. It is perhaps no surprise that in order to quit a place as arcane and complicated as the House of Commons there is a procedure which is both arcane and complicated. Getting there is hard enough, often taking many years of rejection, by both the party and the people, before someone finally arrives in the Commons as a member of Parliament. So why would they ever want to resign?

Sometimes they are in trouble: Eric Illsley, a Labour MP, left in 2011 after being found guilty of fiddling his expenses; Neil Parish, a Conservative MP, had been caught watching porn while searching for tractors online in 2022. Sometimes they just have a better offer: Peter Mandelson left the Commons in 2004 to become a European Commissioner. Boris Johnson went off to become mayor of London in 2008. Robert Kilroy-Silk stopped being a Labour MP so he could go into telly as host of *Day to Day*.

Some just can't face staying: Tony Blair scarpered within hours of standing down as prime minister in 2007, rushing out of the door to spend more time with his money. David Cameron hung around for two months in 2016, before realising it wasn't much fun watching someone else running the country. Johnson jumped before he was pushed in 2023, resigning for the second time as an MP rather than facing the consequences of being found to have misled parliament. Others want to make a point: David Davis, then the Tory shadow home secretary, decided in 2008 to trigger a by-election in protest at the erosion of civil liberties. When the main parties refused to take part in the stunt and did not stand against him he was left to see off two dozen minnows and attention seekers, and returned to the Commons having been easily, pointlessly, re-elected a month later.

The problem for all these MPs, and many, many more, is that once elected you cannot actually resign. There is no handing in your notice to voters, Parliament, the monarch or anyone else. Rules dating back to 1624 ban it, making it clear that 'a man, after he is duly chosen, cannot relinquish'. Back then some MPs were even elected against their will; for most it was a duty and not something to be coveted.

So, in typical parliamentary fashion, when presented with an intractable problem there is an elegant fudge. Officially the only ways in which an MP can be removed from Parliament are death (which is hard to argue with); expulsion by resolution of the House (which is rare; the last one was in 1954); a recall petition (which requires 10 per cent of voters in a seat to demand a by-election); or disqualification.

So an MP who wants out just has to seek disqualification. They could get themselves jailed for more than a year, but that might be a bit extreme and limit post-Parliament employment opportunities. Instead they can accept an office which is deemed to be at odds with being a member of Parliament – in other words one paid by the Crown. MPs cannot be seen to be taking money from the monarch when Parliament should be independent.

So there are two Crown jobs kept on the books; if an MP accepts, they automatically forfeit their seat in the Commons. In a political world packed with questionable roles, these are the ultimate non-jobs. The first is the 'Crown Steward and Bailiff of the three Chiltern Hundreds of Stoke, Desborough and Burnham', which is an old administrative area covering part of Buckinghamshire.

And the other title is the 'Crown Steward and Bailiff of the Manor of Northstead', which is less grand than it sounds. Even in 1600 the 'manor' was a 'lowe house' unfit for habitation. For a time a shepherd lived in it, until it fell down. These days the site of the manor house is thought to be at the bottom of a lake in Peasholm Park, a short walk from the north beach at Scarborough. Today it is an oriental-themed collection of bridges, paths and lakes, with a boathouse, mini golf and a café, acting as a pretty walk from the sea to the town. And it still has a steward and bailiff.

It remains the chancellor of the exchequer's job to appoint an MP to one of these two roles, which they then keep only until someone else wants to resign. The chancellor signs a warrant of appointment, with a witness looking on, and then a letter is sent to the quitter without the letters 'MP' after their name. Ouch.

The two titles alternate, so there is always a vacancy for an outgoing MP to take. It means that Sadiq Khan, Chris Huhne, David Davis, Tony Blair, Betty Boothroyd, Neil Kinnock, Roy Jenkins, John Stonehouse and John Profumo were all stewards of the Chiltern Hundreds (good pub quiz trivia for you) while the subaquatic Manor of Northstead was briefly the responsibility of Cameron, Mandelson, Adams, Eden and Kilroy-Silk, along with John Bercow, David Miliband, Martin McGuinness, Matthew Parris and Enoch Powell. Johnson actually has the rare distinction of having held both offices after resigning twice.

The first MP to become steward of the Chiltern Hundreds is known to be John Pitt in 1751. As for the Manor of Northstead: it's complicated. Lots of accounts suggest that the first steward was Sir George Rose quitting as MP for Christchurch in March 1844, although other records suggest it was Patrick Chalmers, MP for Montrose Burghs, a month earlier, and there was a mix-up in the paperwork. Confirmation that this arcane and complicated procedure has not worked properly since day one.

# 29

# Beach hut, Beaulieu

*Sunday, 24 August 1952*

These days we might worry about the House of Lords being too old, yet when Lord Montagu of Beaulieu inherited his peerage he was aged just two. Aged 10, he stood for hours clutching a black velvet bag full of sandwiches to keep him going while wearing the full regalia of a peer during the coronation of George VI. His biography then reads like that of any member of the British aristocracy – schooled at Eton, then Oxford to study modern history, and then the Grenadier Guards – before an engagement to Anne Gage, an American actress. But he was leading a double life, falling in with what he called a bohemian crowd, admitting years later to being bisexual. And it was his friendship with gay journalist Peter Wildeblood that would catapult him across the front pages, land him in jail, and help bring about the legalisation of homosexuality in Britain.

It is impossible to overstate how bleak, dangerous and illegal it was to be gay in Britain in the 1950s. Winston Churchill as prime minister told ministers in early 1954 that the 'Tory Party won't want to accept responsibility for making law on homosexuality more lenient', according to cabinet papers. Sir David Maxwell Fyfe, who was Churchill's hardline home secretary from 1951 to 1954, vowed to 'rid England of this male vice . . . this plague', telling the House of Commons in December 1953: 'Homosexuals in general are exhibitionists and proselytisers and are a danger to others, especially the young, and so long as I hold the office of Home Secretary I shall give no countenance to the view that they should not be prevented from being such a danger.' On his watch, the number of men jailed for homosexual acts soared to more than 1,000 a year. Alan Turing, the war hero who cracked the Enigma code, had been convicted of gross indecency in 1952. A year later the actor Sir John Gielgud was arrested by an undercover police officer in a public lavatory. Then it was Montagu's turn.

Aged 27 and still the youngest member of the Lords, he was charged along with his cousin Michael Pitt-Rivers, a 36-year-old Dorset farmer, and 30-year-old Wildeblood, with committing unnatural acts and gross indecency with two RAF men, Edward McNally and John Reynolds, who received immunity for testifying against them. It was the journalist Wildeblood who first met McNally in spring 1952 in London while the airman was on leave, and they were alleged to have had sex. Then on a warm Sunday in August 1952 Montagu invited Wildeblood to his beach hut near his Beaulieu estate, overlooking the Solent. Wildeblood brought along McNally and Reynolds, and Pitt-Rivers joined them. Exactly what happened that weekend was disputed. In court, McNally and Reynolds made a series of claims about 'abandoned behaviour' and alleged the other three men performed sex acts. Montagu denied this, breaking half a century of silence in 2007 to tell the London *Evening Standard*: 'We had some drinks, we danced, we kissed, that's all.'

A few weeks later, while some Boy Scouts camped on the Beaulieu estate, Montagu called the police to report a camera had been stolen. Instead of investigating the theft, the police charged him with molesting one of the 14-year-old boys, a crime of which he was later acquitted. But then, on the morning of Saturday, 9 January 1954, the police came for him again, this time in relation to the night at the beach hut. Montagu, Pitt-Rivers and Reynolds were charged with 'conspiracy to incite certain male persons to commit serious offences with male persons', a crime last pursued against Oscar Wilde. The case involving a peer, a journalist and a rural landowner sent shock-waves through Britain. On hearing the news Percy Elland, the editor of the *Evening Standard* at the time, wrote to the paper's owner Lord Beaverbrook: 'Scotland Yard are definitely stepping up their activities against homosexuals.'

Put on trial in March 1954, all three defendants told Winchester Assizes that the offences alleged by the RAF men never happened. Wildeblood was lent long johns by his solicitor so that he would not shiver in the dock and appear afraid. Montagu later said: 'The trial was horrific. Frightening. Terrible. Very traumatic.' From the dock Montagu said there was no truth to the claim that he had any 'sexual relations' with Reynolds, and denied taking him to the bedroom of the beach hut. It was, he said, a complete invention. Yet all three were found guilty of 'consensual homosexual offences'.

Wildeblood and Pitt-Rivers were sentenced to eighteen months in prison. Montagu got twelve months, the judge saying his offences were less serious than the others'. It cost him his engagement, among other things. Montagu's defence lawyer said that were it not for the case, his client would now be a happily married man, describing him as a 'useful member of the House of Lords and a kindly landowner' who now 'was faced with a bitter future'. Maxwell Fyfe, still ensconced in the Home Office, had claimed another high-profile scalp. Yet it was the airmen Reynolds and McNally who were jeered as they left the court, while there were cheers, applause and thumbs-up for the convicted. Public attitudes, it seemed, were changing about what consensual adults were free to do in the privacy of their own homes, or beach huts. It would take a while, though, for politics to catch up.

Indeed, during the trial there were calls in Parliament from the easily shocked Labour MP George Craddock for 'temporary legislation to safeguard public morale by preventing the publication by the Press of gross and unnecessary details in cases of homosexuality'. But it was a plea from another Labour MP, Desmond

Donnelly, in the same debate which had a more lasting impact, calling on Churchill's government to set up a Royal Commission into the full slate of archaic, punitive homosexuality laws. Donnelly went on to raise concerns about 'some of the police methods which have come to light in recent litigation' and warned that some MPs 'are watching this matter very carefully and will not hesitate to expose any case in which they think that the methods of the police have been improper'. Robert Boothby, a Conservative MP, would also argue in favour of decriminalising consensual sex above the age of consent, arguing that jailing gay men was 'not only dangerous, but madness'. Not that they were all great gay rights champions. Boothby also told the Commons: 'The existing laws are outmoded and they do not achieve the objective of all of us, which is to limit the incidence of homosexuality and to mitigate its evil effects.'

In July 1954, just four months after the Montagu case, the government caved and announced that John Wolfenden, a former headmaster and vice-chancellor of the University of Reading, would chair a Royal Commission examining prostitution and homosexuality laws, dating back to the Buggery Act of 1533, which had been passed into law under Henry VIII. Wildeblood was one of three gay men who gave evidence to the committee, which sat sixty-two times over three years. The inquiry produced a 155-page report, which sold thousands of copies and became a bestseller. It recommended that 'homosexual behaviour between consenting adults in private should no longer be considered a criminal offence'. It rejected the idea of homosexuality as an illness, and added: 'It is not, in our view, the function of the law to intervene in the private life of citizens, or to seek to enforce any particular pattern of behaviour.'

The report's proposed changes to prostitution laws were implemented within eighteen months, but the Churchill government rejected the recommendations on homosexuality. On 7 March 1958 *The Times* published a letter, organised by the academic Tony Dyson, calling on the Tory government, now led by Harold

Macmillan, to introduce early legislation decriminalising gay sex between consenting adults. Among the signatories confident that it would 'deserve the widest support from humane men of all parties' were Clement Attlee, the former Labour prime minister, the philosophers Isaiah Berlin and Bertrand Russell, the writer J. B. Priestley and the historian A. J. P. Taylor. It led to the creation of the Homosexual Law Reform Society, which continued to campaign on the issue until the passing of the Sexual Offences Act in 1967, thirteen years after the Montagu case had shocked the country.

As for Montagu himself, after being released from prison he refused to discuss the case for decades, instead throwing himself into rescuing and preserving the Beaulieu estate and becoming a pioneer in the management of stately homes. Asked by the *Evening Standard* about the role he played in the eventual decriminalisation, he said: 'I am slightly proud that the law has been changed to the benefit of so many people. I would like to think that I would get some credit for that.'

# 30

# Sand dunes, Samson, Isles of Scilly

*Tuesday, 10 August 1965*

'Would he care to comment on the trade figures? The Prime Minister crossed one sunburnt leg over the other and surveyed a patch of blue sky.' It was a lucky *Times* correspondent who was despatched to quiz Harold Wilson in August 1965 at a press conference given in the unlikely surroundings of the sand dunes of the Isles of Scilly. 'Forty gently perspiring representatives of the world's press, many of them city-suited and suede-shoed, had stumbled ashore on Samson, a quarter-of-an-hour by boat from the main island of St. Mary, where the Prime Minister has his holiday bungalow,' the sun-kissed reporter went on. And it was here, in between questions about the economy, defence and the prospect of a Labour-Liberal pact, that Wilson became the first prime minister to show his knees in public – and for the benefit of the cameras too – changing forever the idea of our political leaders at rest and on holiday.

The Wilsons had been regulars on the Scillies for years. They liked it so much they built a home there called 'Lowenva', Cornish for 'House of Happiness', a not especially attractive grey-brick, squat, three-bedroom bungalow on the outskirts of Hugh Town, the main settlement on the island of St Mary's. It seems to have been designed specifically as the home of an unassuming man of the people. (After Mary Wilson's death in 2018, the bungalow was put on the market for £425,000, which was later lowered to £395,000 and eventually sold for £375,000.)

Wilson liked island life, the sense of being abroad from Britain while still ostensibly holidaying at home. *Time* magazine reported in 1965: 'The Wilsons have always found the Scillies a grand spot for a quiet holiday, but this year, now that he is PM, Wilson's outing in the sparsely populated isles has looked like a political junket, with all those sweating newspapermen tailing him around, and Foreign Secretary Michael Stewart dropping over from the mainland to talk statecraft.' In fact, Stewart was staying on St Mary's too.

It was Wilson's first summer holiday since becoming PM with a narrow majority in October 1964, ousting Alec Douglas-Home, who belonged not only to a different party but to a different age. Whereas the defeated Conservative had to renounce a peerage to run for office, Wilson was the modern man of the people, all HP Sauce and pipe-smoking (even if he did also enjoy a cigar away from the cameras). Wilson and his team were obsessed with image, modelling much of what he did on John F. Kennedy, who in 1961 became US president as a telegenic moderniser. Wilson would often lift his wedding ring into view and pose as a family man, a subliminal contrast to his new Tory opponent, bachelor Edward Heath.

In the dunes of the unpopulated island of Samson, we see it all: Wilson with pipe in hand, wife Mary in a swimsuit handing out cups of tea, while son Giles plays with an inflatable dinghy. And the PM's shorts: grey, pulled up high to tuck in an open-necked blue shirt, his sandy, sockless feet in sandals. Wilson himself suggested to the gathering photographers that perhaps they might take a 'contemplative shot', and headed off to a rocky outcrop where he could be snapped from all angles, still clutching his pipe.

Looking at the photographs and Pathé newsreel of Wilson at play it is striking how carefully he constructed the image of an everyman, in fact an everydad: unfashionable shorts, a rucksack carrying the day's provisions, popping into the local Co-op on the way to his favourite pub, the Mermaid. With the waves lapping at the beach and seagull cries overhead, the journalists' questions turned to Malaysia's move a couple of days earlier to expel its state of Singapore from the Federation of Malaya following riots. Might the prime minister have to cut short his three-week break on this island paradise? No need to think of it, Wilson assured the sweaty newspapermen. Five days later pressure to do something about Singapore had grown. Crisis talks were called but Wilson refused to go back to London; instead, with Stewart, he hopped over the channel by helicopter only as far as the Culdrose naval base near Penzance on the mainland. Other ministers and Lord Head, Britain's high commissioner in Malaysia, had to travel to Cornwall to meet them. On the way back Wilson stopped off for tea with Frank Cousins, the minister of technology, who was also holidaying nearby. Quite the gang of them. After that, the press left Wilson alone for the rest of his break. It is an agreement that most prime ministers since have reluctantly entered into: one posed snap and then clear off.

It became the model for his successors. From Margaret and Denis Thatcher posing on a beach and playing golf in Cornwall for the benefit of the cameras in 1981 to Tony Blair's walkabouts near whichever celebrity's mansion he had borrowed. By contrast, Gordon Brown struggled with the whole business, once heading to a beach photo op in a jacket and dark trousers before finding any reason to return to Downing Street.

David and Samantha Cameron had it down to a fine art, notably taking time out of their holiday to point at fish in a Cornwall shop in 2011, point at fish in Devon 2012, point at fish in a Portuguese market in 2013, and again point at fish at a different Portuguese fish market in 2014. The reason for the posed picture is simple: to prevent the paparazzi from catching a premier in unguarded holiday mode. Which is precisely what happened to Cameron in 2013 when, during another holiday to Cornwall, he was spotted performing the age-old dad routine of awkwardly wriggling his way out of damp swimming shorts with a Mickey Mouse towel tied around his waist to protect his modesty.

Wilson avoided that fate. In the sand dunes of 1965, the photographers suggested he might take a dip. 'I'm not going in,' he insisted, wagging a finger, before casting doubt on his swimming prowess. 'My style is about as good as the local seals.' And for a prime minister, style, even on holiday, is what really matters.

# 31

# Swimming pool, Cliveden

*Saturday, 8 July 1961*

Even on a cold spring evening, perhaps especially so, the water is delightful. Steam gently rises from the shallow waves. Outdoor pools are just better. None of the stuffy heat and chlorine and noise that you get indoors. And this is a long way from the plasters and hair and screaming that make public swimming baths so awful.

Sploshing about in the most famous pool in politics, surrounded by the high garden walls, gazing up at the ornate water tower installed after the manor house burnt down for the second time in the nineteenth century, it is impossible not to feel the sense of history. Climbing out of the pool to make use of the hot tubs, it is impossible not to feel the cold. It was a much warmer summer's evening in 1961 when Christine Keeler, a 19-year-old model and girl about town, left wet footprints on these same herringboned red-brick tiles. She was dashing to grab a towel, just as a group from the big house arrived to change her life.

Keeler had an unfortunate start. Her father abandoned the family when she was young. Her mother set up home with another man, living in a converted railway carriage at Wraysbury in Berkshire, without electricity or hot water. After leaving school without any qualifications, she moved to London aged 15. It was while working at Murray's Cabaret Club in Soho that she met Stephen Ward, a slightly dubious osteopath to the stars, and Mandy Rice-Davies, a showgirl from Wales. The two young women moved into Ward's house in Marylebone, and the partying went up a notch.

Lord Astor liked a party too. The third viscount, the eldest son of Nancy Astor, who was the first woman to take her seat in the Commons, was one of Ward's high-society patients. A former Conservative MP, he was a ministerial bag carrier in Chamberlain's 1930s government, served as a naval intelligence officer in the Second World War, and had to give up the Commons when he inherited the peerage from his father in 1952. Having suffered an injury after falling while hunting, he did what anyone with a bad back would do and gave his osteopath the use of a cottage in the grounds of his stately home in the Berkshire countryside. Spring Cottage was a nice quiet spot, and long before Ward moved in had previously been used by the Duchess of Sutherland to entertain Queen Victoria.

Two worlds – of stiff-upper-lipped English aristocracy and the sexually-charged sixties – would collide one July weekend in 1961. Ward had invited a gang to the cottage for a party, including Keeler and Yevgeny Ivanov, a Soviet naval attaché and spy. A mile away, Astor also had friends to stay. Among the first to arrive were John Profumo, the suave secretary of state for war in Macmillan's Conservative government, and his wife, Valerie Hobson, a 1940s film actress. Among the other two dozen guests on the Saturday night were Nubar Gulbenkian, a flamboyant Armenian tycoon and socialite who travelled in a custom-made gold-plated taxi, and Lord Mountbatten, the war hero and uncle of Prince Philip.

The story of what happened next is as famous as it is famously unreliable. The problem with a saga of sex and lies is that everyone involved lies about everything, including the sex. Lies in the papers, lies in the courtroom, lies in the Commons.

So Ward and Keeler were in the pool. Or maybe just Keeler, who was skinny-dipping. Or was wearing a costume, but it was too big and falling off. Or it had been taken and hidden by Ward. At around 10.30 p.m. Astor and his guests, in dinner suits and evening gowns, left Cliveden House for a stroll. To take in the evening air. Or perhaps to admire the small bronze statue of Astor's son riding a dolphin which had recently been installed at the pool edge at the deep end of the pool. In politics, as in life, timing is everything. And just as Profumo walked into the walled garden he caught a glimpse of Keeler, naked. Someone, possibly Valerie Profumo, helped Keeler find a towel. Astor said that nothing more happened that night. When Keeler sold her story eighteen months later she claimed Astor and Profumo had chased her naked around the pool.

On Sunday the president of Pakistan, General Ayub Khan, joined the guests for lunch. Keeler claimed in the papers that there were more pool-based frolics: the men with a girl each on their shoulders, trying to wrestle their opponents into the water. Keeler was on Profumo's shoulders. Or maybe not. At some point Profumo acquired Keeler's telephone number, and an affair ensued. Then there was also Ivanov, who drove her back to London and went to bed with her. She was sleeping with a Russian spy and a government minister at the same time. Or actually probably not. It now seems clear that the fling with Ivanov ended months before the Profumo one began. When it did, Keeler claimed as part of her insatiable desire to overshare with papers that she cooked sausages for the minister before they had sex in front of the television. She described their affair memorably as a 'very, very well-mannered screw of convenience'.

This was at a time when Russia, via Ivanov, wanted Britain's military secrets, and Profumo was a man who kept them. Ward was said to have asked Keeler to obtain secrets – whether government or personal – from Profumo. A secret camera might have been used by the Russian to take pictures of Keeler and Profumo together. Or might not. Ivanov might have bugged Keeler's flat. Or might not. If the Russians had not directly got useful government information through Keeler, they probably had got enough dirt to blackmail Profumo into handing over the good stuff. Whatever the veracity of the claims and counter-claims, the affair was all a bit too messy for the government, and in August 1961 Sir Norman Brook, the cabinet secretary, told Profumo to get out of it.

Profumo dashed off a note to Keeler: 'Darling, . . . Alas something's blown up tomorrow night and I can't therefore make it . . . I leave the next day for various trips and then a holiday so won't be able to see you again until some time in September. Blast it. Please take great care of yourself and don't run away. Love J.' And that was the end of it.

Except it wasn't. More trouble came to Keeler's door in 1962, when her jilted ex Johnny Edgecombe turned up outside Ward's place, shooting a semi-automatic pistol. His arrest and subsequent trial meant the police began looking into Ward's other connections, and the whole thing unravelled. The gossip press started nibbling at the story, until it reached the national papers. The rumours also reached Downing Street. 'I was forced to spend a great deal of today over a silly scrape (women this time, thank God, not boys) into which one of the ministers has got himself,' prime minister Harold Macmillan wrote in his diary on 15 March 1963, mentioning the Profumo affair for the first time. The PM suggested it would not matter if it was just the sex, but it was a tale of national security too, bringing together Astor and Ivanov. 'This is the new Cliveden set!' Indeed it was.

More stories appeared in the press, and then MPs raised questions in Parliament. On 22 March 1963 Profumo made a personal statement to the Commons, outing himself as the person at the centre of what he called 'rumours connecting a minister with a Miss Keeler and a recent trial at the Central Criminal Court'. 'My wife and I first met Miss Keeler at a house party in July, 1961, at Cliveden,' he said. 'Among a number of people there was Dr Stephen Ward, whom we already knew slightly, and a Mr Ivanov, who was an attaché at the Russian Embassy.'

He went on: 'Between July and December, 1961, I met Miss Keeler on about half a dozen occasions at Dr Ward's flat, when I called to see him and his friends. Miss Keeler and I were on friendly terms. There was no impropriety whatsoever in my acquaintanceship with Miss Keeler.' This, of course, was not true. In an audacious move he added: 'I shall not hesitate to issue writs for libel and slander if scandalous allegations are made or repeated outside the House.'

But then the lies all unravelled. By 5 April he confirmed the affair, destroying his political career. By mid-June he had resigned as an MP. The press had a field day: a hot summer of saucy speculation about other ministers, royals, celebrities. The opposition made hay too. Harold Wilson, the Labour leader, took the scandal to the Commons on 17 June, declaring: 'This is a debate without precedent in the annals of this House. It arises from disclosures which have shocked the moral conscience of the nation.' Wilson talked salaciously about 'clear evidence of a sordid underworld network'.

Macmillan replied that 'what has happened has inflicted a deep, bitter, and lasting wound', adding: 'I do not remember in the whole of my life, or even in the political history of the past, a case of a Minister of the Crown who has told a deliberate lie to his wife, to his legal advisers and to his Ministerial colleagues, not once but over and over again, who has then repeated this lie to the House of Commons.'

Lord Denning was asked to carry out an inquiry into the mess. While its conclusion – that there was no security risk and the fault lay with Profumo and his lie to the Commons – was dismissed by some as a whitewash, the eye-popping detail in his 60,000-word report made it a bestseller, with 4,000 copies sold to the public in its first hour, rising to 100,000 over the following months. It was described as the 'raciest and most readable Blue Book ever published', discrediting those at the top of an already tired Establishment personified by Macmillan, who resigned through ill-health days before Denning published.

Ward was charged with living off the immoral earnings of prostitutes. During the trial more accounts, claims and lies emerged. At Marylebone magistrates' court, defence counsel James Burge asked Mandy Rice-Davies about her claims to have slept with Astor: 'Do you know Lord Astor has made a statement to the police saying that these allegations of yours are absolutely untrue?' Rice-Davies replied: 'Well he would, wouldn't he?'

Distraught, Ward, abandoned by his society friends, took an overdose during the trial, was convicted in his absence, but died on 3 August 1963 without coming out of a coma. Keeler was jailed for nine months for perjury, and served six months. The defining image of Keeler was of her posing naked on an iconic Arne Jacobsen curved butterfly chair, photographed by David Bailey. Except it was taken by Lewis Morley. She wasn't naked. The photo was taken to promote a film which was never released. And the chair was a cheap replica, which now sits in the Victoria and Albert Museum, a fitting monument to a scandal where nothing was quite what it seemed.

What is remarkable sixty years on is the endurance of what is an unremarkable, if enjoyably bawdy, sex scandal. Cliveden still rather enjoys its licentious association, hosting Profumo-themed dinners and even serving a scandalously tasty Profumo cocktail (gin, lychee liqueur, strawberry liqueur and pink champagne), although it is unclear if he ever actually drank a drop of it. In fact, the only thing about this tale which is crystal-clear is the water in the swimming pool. For the avoidance of doubt, I kept my trunks on throughout. But then I would say that, wouldn't I?

# 32

# Log Flume, Flambards

*Monday, 4 August 1997*

Ferdi is a Cornish legend. Children queue to have their photos taken with him, mums get a hug while reluctant dads make awkward high-fives. A six-foot fox already stands out in a crowd, but this cuddly mascot takes it further, combining a bright-red waistcoat with big, cool-dude sunglasses, which is far from the most embarrassing thing anyone has worn to the Flambards theme park in Helston, Cornwall.

That honour goes to William Hague and his baseball cap. He had been Conservative leader for less than eight weeks, and hoped to shake off the fusty, staid image of a party which had suffered a devastating election loss and instead get down with the kids who had fallen for the Cool Britannia vibes of New Labour. So Hague went to Flambards and met Ferdi himself. He also fell for the old adage that if you want to get ahead, get a hat. Specifically, a hat with his name on it. Unfortunately, this was at a time when polls showed nobody knew who he was, so this seemed less like a brand extension and more like a name badge when meeting strangers. It had 'Hague' on the front and 'A fresh future' on the back. Trendy. The stunt was the first leg of a two-month 'listening tour' of Britain designed to re-engage the public with a tired party which had just been shown the door after eighteen years in power. And it started in Cornwall.

Flambards played a big part in my childhood around this time too. A lot of summer holidays to St Austell meant a lot of trips to the family theme park, which first opened in 1976, combining your standard funfair rides with 'Britain in the Blitz', a creepy mock-up of a musty, bomb-damaged street which could really worry a 10-year-old. In keeping with my memories of those 1990s holidays, Hague's day out was accompanied by torrential rain.

At the 1997 election the Tories lost all three of their seats in Cornwall, including David Harris's seat of St Ives, home to Flambards, which went to Labour, and neighbouring Falmouth and Camborne, where Seb Coe lost to the Lib Dems. It was Coe's idea to go to Flambards, so the then 40-year-old chief of staff joined Harris, then 59, and 36-year-old Hague in the log flume for the youthful photo opp which came to define his spell as leader. Days later Conservative Central Office announced that they were to sell the Hague caps for £7, in response to er . . . overwhelming popular demand. Or, as *The Independent* reported at the time: 'Mr Hague's fashion statement, interpreted as part of his bid to woo young voters, has been successful in inspiring at least one letter from a young Conservative requesting a cap.'

At the time the photocall made only a modest splash in the next day's papers. A photo of the three men in a boat only got page seven in the Tory Party's in-house paper, *The Daily Telegraph*, which went with the Queen Mother's birthday for its page-one pic. It did make the front page of both *The Independent* (a twenty-six-word caption with the pun 'Tory wet') and *The Guardian*, under the headline 'Tory leader takes the plunge', although inside the paper Katharine Viner warned: 'You can never make a nerd look cool, whatever tricks you pull.' Radio Cornwall branded Hague 'Man at C&A'.

However, Hague himself thinks it only came to be seen as a vote-losing gaffe with hindsight. He once told me: 'These things become part of the narrative later, after the event. This can happen in any public job – if it starts not to go well, whatever photocall you did in the past suddenly starts to look very embarrassing. You have to try and anticipate that and avoid those situations.' It was, he says, symptomatic of the problem for opposition parties struggling to gain attention, especially in the wake of an election wipeout when the government is riding high in the polls. 'Don't worry about grabbing publicity or the photo each day. You just have to live with the frustration that you're not always in the media and that you can't always command attention. Don't do anything unwise to try and grab that attention, I think, is the moral of that particular episode.' His advice to any other leader of the opposition told to don a baseball cap is blunt: 'Don't do it.'

The image, though, endured. Many, wrongly, remember Hague also wearing a baseball cap backwards to the Notting Hill Carnival a couple of weeks after the Flambards trip. In fact on that occasion he was hatless, wearing chinos and a blue shirt to drink milk from a halved coconut. Fashion advice, though, seemed to dominate Hague's leadership. In 1998 he hired John Morgan, a senior editor at *GQ* and author of *Debrett's New Guide to Etiquette & Modern Manners*, to advise him on dress code. A year later Hague told his Conservative colleagues to take off their ties, while Francis Maude, his shadow chancellor, took to doing interviews in shirtsleeves. A leaked memo revealed details of 'Project Hague' to overhaul his image with a series of photo opportunities, including evening walks on the beach, practising judo with the Army, and even abseiling. None of it, of course, worked. At the 2001 election, the Tories made a net gain of just one seat, and that wasn't in Cornwall. Hague's fox had been shot. Ferdi, by contrast, lives on to this day.

# Food and drink

# 33

# Dining room, Warwick House

*Wednesday, 11 July 1962*

If you want a friend in politics, get a dog. And if you want a good story, get a lunch. The events of summer 1962 reveal how these truisms still hold in politics today, even if a loose-lipped, booze-fuelled lunch in these more abstemious times is even harder to come by than loyalty.

Harold Macmillan had spent five and a half years as Conservative prime minister carefully cultivating an unflappable image of unshowy control, in contrast to his more flamboyant, risk-taking predecessor Anthony Eden, who had stepped down in 1955. Having declared that 'Most of our people have never had it so good' in 1957, Macmillan won the 1959 election promising 'Life's better under the Conservatives', increasing his majority in the Commons from 60 to 100. A relaxed, One Nation Old Etonian, presiding over a growing parliamentary party – no wonder Macmillan is often compared to chillaxing David Cameron.

By 1962, however, things were not looking so good. The Conservatives had sensationally lost the Orpington by-election in March to the Liberals, one of the biggest upsets in British political history. Then in June the Conservatives lost Middlesbrough West to Labour. But these were not the cause of Macmillan's pain, just the symptoms. The economy was stalling, with pay held low and deflation a real risk. Selwyn Lloyd, who had been

Macmillan's chancellor of the exchequer for two years, had imposed a deeply unpopular 'Pay Pause', effectively banning pub-lic-sector wage rises, while also introducing controversial meas-ures like a 15 per cent tax on sweets, ice-cream and fizzy drinks in what became known as the Lollipop Budget.

Cabinet pressure had been growing for a change in economic policy, and a change in chancellor. Iain Macleod, the Conserva-tive Party chairman, and Rab Butler, the home secretary, were pressing Macmillan for a more expansionist approach to stimulate the economy ahead of the 1964 election. Lloyd had resisted the idea of going for growth, a position that had actually been backed repeatedly by the cabinet. However there were complaints that Lloyd was too concerned about the risk of inflation, and had not 'put over' the government's policies well enough. Macmillan had multiple reasons for a reshuffle, not all of them contradictory. He was frustrated by his chancellor – who had become 'an immense human and political problem' – and had found himself trying to run economic policy himself. He thought nurses, university teach-ers and probation workers should get pay rises. He needed the economy to bounce back before a general election. After a decade of Tory rule, the public could become bored and want a change. His government, he feared, was looking old and tired.

The problem was that Macmillan and Lloyd were old friends: the prime minister had allowed his ally the use of Chequers, the PM's grace-and-favour property, because he already had his own country house at Birch Grove. Lloyd's black Labrador (who had the now-un-PC name Sambo) had the run of the place. The dog was Lloyd's closest companion following his painful divorce from his wife, Bae, in 1957. The two men, both prone to bouts of loneliness, had shared their private hopes and fears over the years, but now they too were increasingly estranged and heading for a split.

In the summer of 1962 Macmillan wrote in his diary of Lloyd being a 'true and loyal friend' who 'seems to me to have lost grip'. But even as he concluded that he must remove him, Macmillan added that 'it will be personally terrible' and 'I will be accused of gross disloyalty.' He wasn't wrong. But what to do with Lloyd instead? He had already been foreign secretary. His opposition to capital punishment meant he was unsuited to the role of home secretary, who still signed off recommendations to the monarch of the prerogative of mercy. Anything else would be a demotion. So he had to go, and – in a second terrible decision – Macmillan felt it would soften the blow if others went with him. Squeamish about what needed doing, he resolved to put it off until the autumn.

And so to lunch. Newspaper magnate Lord Rothermere was hosting at his home, Warwick House, a gleaming white palatial property in smart St James's. Built by Henry Herrington in 1771, it was at one time furnished with crimson velvet curtains made from a Delhi Durbar tent. With views of Green Park, and a stone's throw from Buckingham Palace, it was close to the epi-centre of the London social scene. Rothermere's third child, and first son, Vere, was born in the house during a dinner party in 1925, with guests, including Winston Churchill, invited upstairs to greet the baby. Over the next three decades Warwick House was party central, with royalty and stars of stage and screen rub-bing shoulders with artists like Lucian Freud and Francis Bacon, all under the watchful eye of Rothermere's socialite wife Ann, who eventually left him in 1952 for Ian Fleming of James Bond fame after a long, passionate, not terribly secret affair.

Now single, Rothermere preferred a quieter life (although he mixed a mean Martini) and used the dining room for rather more strait-laced business, favouring the company of captains of indus-try, politicians, indeed anyone who could help his newspapers. Warwick House was so big, the story goes, that if a soufflé was being served the staff had to form a relay to carry the plates sev-eral floors from the basement kitchens up to the dining room before the whole thing sagged.

Political intrigue and gossip was on the menu on Wednesday, 11 July 1962. Rothermere had invited Butler, the home secretary, alongside Walter Terry, the bespectacled political correspondent on the *Daily Mail*, which Rothermere owned. Butler spilt the beans on the reshuffle plans. The next day, under the headline 'MAC'S MASTER PLAN', the paper reported of a planned cabinet clear-out in the autumn, including Lloyd being packed off with a peerage as Lord Chancellor.

The cooked-up plan collapsed like a soufflé. It meant that Macmillan could not wait until the autumn. The reshuffle would instead take place at a speed which would match its brutality. That night he met Lloyd in his temporary office, Admiralty House (like the cabinet, Downing Street was undergoing a major overhaul). For forty-five minutes Macmillan laid out the case for the 'reconstruction' of his government. Lloyd warned, presciently, that it would look like panic, and could lead to calls for the 'old man' prime minister to go. Macmillan suggested his friend might take a peerage, or the chairmanship of Martin's Bank. Lloyd declined both, and left. By a cruel coincidence, that night he had been invited to dinner at Warwick House – scene of the lunch which sealed his fate – where this time Rothermere was hosting the French ambassador, who would no doubt have been very particular about the soufflé.

By this point the evening papers, and early editions of the next morning's, were filled with speculation about major cabinet changes. Macmillan had to act. 'I decided to get on with the reconstruction without any delay,' he wrote in his diary. In total seven cabinet ministers were sent packing. Lloyd, days from his fifty-eighth birthday, was replaced as chancellor by Reginald Maudling, a man thirteen years his junior but still a veteran of the governments of Churchill, Eden and Macmillan.

To keep up the pretence that this was about renewing a younger, fresher party, Macmillan, who was himself 68, tried to ensure that each replacement was younger than his predecessor. Viscount Kilmuir, 62, was swiftly replaced as Lord Chancellor by Lord Dilhorne, 56. Kilmuir grumbled that a cook would get more notice of being sacked. 'It's easier to get Lord Chancellors these days than cooks,' Macmillan replied. Then the dominoes started to fall: David Eccles, 57, was out as education secretary for Peter Thorneycroft, 52; John Maclay, 56, was sacked as Scottish secretary for Michael Noble, 49; Charles Hill, 58, was out from Housing and Local Government for Keith Joseph, 44; and Percy Mills, 72, replaced as minister without portfolio by William Deedes, 49. It wasn't perfect: Harold Watkinson, 52, was replaced as defence secretary by Peter Thorneycroft, who was actually six months older. Earldoms and Orders of the Companions of Honour were bandied about to sweeten the miserable process. 'It was a dreadful day,' Macmillan reflected.

All major reshuffles since have been compared with Macmillan's Night of the Long Knives. Margaret Thatcher, who hailed Macmillan after his death as both an 'idealist' and 'shrewd', learnt the lesson and took her time in executing her clear-outs over several years. Tony Blair's 2006 reshuffle, after a round of dire local election results, saw twelve cabinet jobs chop and change hands, but only Charles Clarke actually left. In 2013, when David Cameron changed up the coalition government, with nine mostly junior ministers leaving and younger women replacing older men from the shires, it was dubbed the 'Night of the Long Drives'. Eight months later Cameron sacked a Macmillan-matching seven cabinet ministers. Unlike Macmillan, Cameron went on to win the general election the following year, increasing the number of Tory MPs to secure a surprise majority. Maybe brutal reshuffling is something they teach at Eton: when Boris Johnson arrived in Downing Street in 2019 he sacked eleven cabinet ministers, four more resigned and two retired in what *The Sun* called the 'Night of the Blond Knives'. Johnson, though, was clearing out Theresa May's ministers.

What was so brutal about 1962 was that Macmillan was knifing his own. When it was officially announced at 7 p.m. on Friday, 14 July all hell broke loose. 'This is a political massacre which can only be interpreted as a gigantic admission of failure,' said Labour leader Hugh Gaitskell, who added that the whole cabinet should have been sacked. Jeremy Thorpe, the Liberal MP, captured it rather more biblically: 'Greater love hath no man than this, that he lay down his friends for his life.'

The sense of panic fatally undermined Macmillan's unruffled reputation; the infantry officer shot in the hand during the First World War had now shot himself in the foot. The unflappable had been caught flapping. He had shown himself to be impulsive, nervy, disloyal. The reshuffle also gave a focal point for the various disparate groups already unhappy with him for hitherto unconnected reasons.

At the next session of PMQs the following Tuesday, both sides cheered when Lloyd entered the Commons chamber. There was stony silence from the Tory benches when Macmillan arrived a few minutes later. His style, belonging more to the Edwardian age than the swinging sixties, went from being his strength to his weakness. The Profumo affair in 1963 further tainted the Establishment of which Macmillan was clearly a part. In October that year, under pressure to resign and laid low with prostate problems, he finally quit as prime minister from his hospital bed, recommending to the Queen that she send for Alec Douglas-Home and not Butler, before standing down as an MP soon after. By contrast, far from leaving politics, Lloyd remained in the Commons, joining Home's cabinet as Commons leader, and in 1971 becoming Commons Speaker for five years before finally taking a peerage.

And so to the dog. When Lloyd was sacked, he had nowhere to keep his pet so Sambo remained at Chequers in the care of the great house's curator, Kathleen Hill. Two weeks after the Night of the Long Knives, Macmillan assembled his new team on the Chequers terrace to talk election tactics late into the evening. As the prime minister spoke, the lonely black Labrador walked slowly among the men looking, forlornly, for his missing master. He stopped in front of the prime minister. Macmillan ignored the dog.

# 34

# Plough Inn, Cadsden

*Saturday, 17 February 1974*

Pubs and politics have gone together since the first Roman drinking houses appeared 2,000 years ago, where thirsts could be quenched while putting the world to rights. However, the heady mixture of power and alcohol can sometimes prove too much. History is littered with ministers and aides losing things while enjoying a drink. Normally, it is laptops, mobile phones and some dignity that are mislaid. Sometimes it can be worse: Tony Blair found out his dream of Britain joining the euro was lost in 1997, when he called Charlie Whelan, Gordon Brown's spin doctor, who was busily, boozily briefing Treasury opposition from his spot in Whitehall's notorious Red Lion. Whelan at least put down his white-wine spritzer to take the call from the furious prime minister. In 2008 Rhodri Glyn Thomas, a Plaid Cymru member of the Welsh Assembly, lost his job as minister for heritage after walking into a Cardiff pub while puffing on a cigar – breaking the ban on smoking he voted into law a year earlier.

And of course there is David Cameron, who left his daughter in a pub. In May 2012 the Camerons were staying at Chequers and had popped down to the local, the Plough Inn in nearby Cadsden. When they left, the PM went in one car with his bodyguards while his wife, Samantha, and their children were in a separate vehicle. 'Sam thought the PM had Nancy, the PM thought Sam had Nancy,' a Downing Street aide explained. Nobody, it transpired, had Nancy.

Cameron once told me that this ranked high on his list of prime ministerial gaffes. 'The one that worried me the most obviously was leaving Nancy in the pub, because for that one moment you do have a total fear about what has happened,' he said. 'But she was incredibly relaxed about it. She was behind the bar, you know, pulling the pints and helping out. And still to this day she has the cartoon in her bedroom, which has her sitting on a bar stool with her head in her hands saying, "Oh my God, I don't know what's going to happen. I've left my father running the country."'

In fact a Conservative prime minister lost something much worse in that same pub. In 1974 Edward Heath lost the election after popping out for a pint. For four years he had been wrestling with the twin perils of Europe and the economy. Having taken Britain into the Common Market in 1973 in the face of major opposition, he was entangled in serious economic and industrial unrest. Miners wanted big pay rises, and when Heath refused they went on strike. A state of emergency was declared, and the shortage of coal meant that soon Britain was forced into a three-day week with power rationed, which not even Patrick Jenkin's ablutions in the dark could prevent. In an attempt to secure a mandate to fight back, on 7 February Heath announced a snap general election for three weeks' time. He told the country: 'This time of strife has got to stop. Only you can stop it. It is time for you to speak, with your vote.' Against the worst economic backdrop for an election since the Great Depression, the Conservatives framed it as the 'Who governs Britain?' vote, asking the public to put the government firmly in control over the 'extremists, the militants, and the plain and simply misguided'. However, the public did not seem to agree. By the halfway point of the campaign, some polling suggested that the Tory advantage was shrinking. Surveys by Harris for the *Daily Express* showed that an eleven-point lead had halved to just 5.5 points in only five days.

Keen to show that all was well, on 17 February Heath invited his top ministers and advisers to Chequers for a strategy meeting. That morning the prime minister took Lord Carrington, his Conservative Party chairman and energy secretary, yomping across the countryside to the Plough Inn for a pre-lunch drink. On the way they stopped for totally natural chats with supportive locals, Heath posing hand on hip leaning on the front gate of Mrs Kathleen Holbrook's Plough Cottage. It was supposed to have been a day off from Conservative campaigning, but 'somebody had remembered to tell the television and newspaper cameramen,' the front page of *The Times* reported, sarcastically. It was such a badly kept secret that a horse rider spent an hour in the saddle waiting outside the pub to catch a glimpse of the Tory premier.

The media loved it. *The Birmingham Post* described him as 'the man with an appetite for work and relaxation'. The *Hull Daily Mail* reported that he had 'walked half a mile through a muddy field' to tell 'newsmen that the public was grasping his party's message'. Once inside the Plough the prime minister drank half-pints of bitter for the photographers, then he went outside and took yet more questions, all on camera, in an attempt to project just how intensely relaxed he was in classic Sunday casual dress. *The Times* said he was wearing a 'heavy blue yachtsman's sweater'. *The Telegraph* went further, claiming he was 'wearing a couple of sweaters'.

As reporters asked how the campaign was going, Carrington said he had no complaints beyond being 'ill-shod for rural walks' and Heath having walked too fast. 'I think the first ten days have gone extremely well,' Heath insisted. 'There won't be any changes of strategy because the issues are absolutely paramount.' Perhaps there should have been. The Tory campaign struggled against the unfortunate economic news and worse political interventions, with Enoch Powell, the former Conservative cabinet minister, announcing he was standing down and urging people to vote Labour to oppose the Common Market. Then, days before polling day, Campbell Adamson, the head of the CBI business group, spoke out against Heath's handling of the strikes, claiming that the Industrial Relations Act had 'sullied every relationship between employers and unions at national level'.

On 28 February, polling day, Labour gained 14 seats, taking them to 301, 17 short of a majority, but now the biggest party over Heath's Conservatives, who were down 28 to 297. So a hung parliament. Heath tried to strike a coalition deal with Jeremy Thorpe's Liberals, but this collapsed. And on Monday, 4 March Labour's Harold Wilson became prime minister for the second time. Heath's gamble had failed. As it turned out, it might have been better to come up with some 'changes of strategy' rather than popping out for half a bitter.

As for the Plough Inn, it has continued to be used by prime ministers and their staff over the years. In 2015 Cameron popped in for fish and chips with China's President Xi Jinping, sealing their 'golden friendship' with a pint of Greene King IPA. The place became a huge hit with Chinese tourists, and a year later it emerged that it had been bought by SinoFortone Investment, a Chinese state-backed enterprise which pumped billions into British projects and talked about rolling out British-style pubs in China. All of which would have pleased Heath: his first major foreign foray after leaving office was to China in May 1974, the first of dozens of visits over three decades. Trips he surely enjoyed more than that ill-advised muddy half-mile stroll to his local, where he left his majority behind.

# 35

# Champany Inn, Linlithgow

*Saturday, 10 July 2004*

The current incarnation of the Scottish Parliament first sat in 1999 in the General Assembly Hall of the Church of Scotland on Edinburgh's Royal Mile, before moving – three years later than planned – into its purpose-built home at Holyrood, designed by Spanish architect Enric Miralles, a modernist tangle of glass, stone, stainless steel and oak.

Yet the fate of Scotland and its place in the Union has perhaps been more influenced by events at the Champany Inn, about forty minutes' drive from central Edinburgh, but it could be a world away. The pub is a seventeenth-century converted cow shed or byre, which for four decades has served up some of the best steaks in Scotland. 'Pub' does not really do it justice. This is hearty fine dining, where a T-bone will set you back £40, before you've added a bottle of their own-branded wine.

The Gothic calligraphy of the Champany logo is not confined to the wine bottles; it's on the signage, the menus, the chair covers, even repeated in gold across the blue carpet. This gem in the West Lothian countryside is the sort of place you go to make a splash, and spend some cash. Two things that Alex Salmond has always enjoyed doing.

It was here on Saturday, 10 July 2004 that he invited an old friend to lunch, and changed the course of political history like few meals before or since. The SNP was in a mess. Salmond's successor as party leader, John Swinney, had resigned after losing eight seats in the Scottish Parliament, one seat in the House of Commons and making no gains in European Parliament elections. Attempts to weaponise opposition to Tony Blair's Iraq War had come to nothing.

If Swinney was underwhelming, the contest to replace him was worse. The favourite was Roseanna Cunningham, who had been Swinney's deputy during the bad years and fallen flat during TV outings. Also running were Michael Russell, who had lost his Holyrood seat under Swinney, and Nicola Sturgeon, who had been an MSP for just five years and was only 33.

Salmond had been SNP leader for a decade from 1990, but since quitting in 2000 had seemed content enjoying the life – and the hospitality – of an MP in Westminster. He had repeatedly rejected the idea of returning, quoting Union Army General William Sherman, who had ruled out running for US president after the American Civil War: 'If nominated I'll decline. If drafted I'll defer. And if elected I'll resign.' However, Salmond was characteristically more than happy to have people try to persuade him otherwise.

He invited Sturgeon, whom he was publicly backing, for a steak and a chat at the restaurant owned by his old friends Anne and Clive Davidson. If he hoped for a quiet early-evening meal away from prying eyes, he had not counted on the Champany Inn hosting a wedding reception. Amid the revelry, this political couple had much to discuss. Surrounded by vast oil paintings hung on the bare-brick walls, with tall candlesticks dripping wax as the small talk went on, Salmond eventually came out with it: would Sturgeon quit the leadership race, and back him instead? She asked for forty-eight hours to think about it. She took only twenty-four before agreeing.

After the weekend of plotting, Salmond returned to Westminster and busied himself with a debate in the Commons on the Butler Review of the Labour government's flawed intelligence on

Saddam Hussein's weapons of mass destruction. He spent much of it teasing his opponents, including claiming that when left-wing Labour MP Bob Marshall-Andrews rose to speak Blair had a look on his face of 'exasperation, consternation and dislike . . . I also detected a look of fear'. Salmond said the matter of Iraq went beyond the 'normal argy-bargy of politics', with thousands of people dead. 'That is the blood price that is being paid for the prime minister's actions,' Salmond declared. 'He has played with other people's chips, and he has done so in a disastrous fashion.' And then he went home to Scotland.

It was exactly the sort of bravura performance that Swinney, and those seeking to replace him, were not capable of producing. The SNP were crying out for some Salmond showboating. They did not have to wait long. The following morning the news broke that he was running to lead them again. 'I changed my mind,' he said, matter-of-factly.

What followed is extraordinary. With Sturgeon by his side as deputy – a fresher but less experienced face and sixteen years his junior – the duo transformed Scottish politics. Within three years he had replaced Labour to become first minister. By 2011 the SNP had a majority in Holyrood, something the proportional voting system was supposed to render all but impossible.

This overwhelming mandate led to the 2014 referendum on Scottish independence, finally testing the SNP dream exactly eighty years after the party was founded. In April 2011, just ahead of the SNP securing that majority, a YouGov poll found that only 28 per cent of people supported independence, 57 per cent were opposed and the rest did not know or would not vote. In the referendum which took place three and a half years later, 45 per cent voted in favour of Scotland going it alone, and that was only after the combined forces of the UK coalition government, Conservatives, Labour, Lib Dems and endless Gordon Brown speeches had been thrown at the panicking cause of unionism. David Cameron later let slip that the Queen 'purred down the line' when he called to let her know her country was still intact. The morning after the vote, after a second decade as leader and seven years as first minister, Salmond quit again. Looking drained, he told reporters: 'I think that we have to understand and recognise when it is time to give someone else a chance to move that forward.'

That someone was Sturgeon. She was the only candidate, elected unopposed as SNP leader. Salmond, meanwhile, was heading back to the Champany Inn, running up a £1,000 taxpayer-funded bill for a steak and oysters golfing dinner less than a week after he announced his resignation.

Sturgeon, meanwhile, would go on to take the SNP to greater heights still, becoming the first first minister to serve a third term, overtaking Salmond's record of longevity, and winning 56 out of Scotland's 59 MPs in the 2015 general election. Nothing, though, lasts forever. And the higher they fly, the harder they fall.

After aborted attempts to force the Westminster government into granting a second independence referendum and a huge public row over plans to make it easier for people to legally change their gender, Sturgeon suddenly quit as SNP leader in February 2023. Within days of leaving office the party was engulfed in a police investigation over funding. She went on to be arrested, along with her husband and former SNP chief executive Peter Murrell, and the treasurer Colin Beattie. All three were released without charge pending further investigation. In one striking image, police erected a tent in Sturgeon's front garden – a scene more reminiscent of a murder. In fact it was just the SNP's untarnishable reputation that was being buried.

As for Salmond, after taking up the questionable offer of a chat show on Russian state-controlled RT, in 2018 he became embroiled in a series of sexual assault allegations dating from when he was first minister in 2013. Two years later he was cleared of all charges, having always maintained his innocence from the moment the claims first emerged in the *Daily Record*.

Within hours of the story breaking in August 2018 he had called an impromptu press conference. Yes, back at the Champany Inn.

Salmond sat in the wedding marquee, surrounded by champagne boxes, and addressed the somewhat baffled groups of reporters. He admitted that he was 'no saint' but denied 'any semblance of criminality'. Oh, and he announced that he was taking the Scottish government – the government of his protégé Sturgeon – to court for its 'fundamentally flawed' handling of the case. A judge later ruled that the government's inquiries had been 'unlawful in respect that they were procedurally unfair and that they were tainted with apparent bias'. Having cleared his name, Salmond went on to set up the Alba Party as a rival pro-independence outfit to Sturgeon's SNP. In the months and years that followed the war of words between these once-great allies was as bloody as the Champany's steaks that first sealed their leadership deal.

# 36

# Lock Keeper's Inn, Belfast

*Thursday, 28 August 2008*

Hillary Clinton was on her way to Honolulu when she was sent the email explaining why the Northern Ireland peace process was threatened because a 59-year-old homophobe had been caught shagging the 19-year-old owner of a café which she secretly helped to bankroll. The US secretary of state had received a memo from her longtime confidant Sidney Blumenthal, which warned: 'The political crisis in Northern Ireland is fast moving and fluid.' He wasn't wrong.

Life in Northern Ireland is a constant, careful balancing act between competing forces across politics and religion. But the fragile, if dull, façade was shattered by an extraordinary story of sex, money and God, a thoroughly modern scandal from a province so often trapped in its past.

It begins with the death of a butcher. Billy McCambley was an old friend of Iris Robinson, a Democratic Unionist Party triple-hatted powerhouse who served as an MP in Westminster, an MLA in the Stormont Assembly and a councillor in Castlereagh. Before McCambley's death in February 2008 she promised to look after his only son, Kirk. She did more than that. She embarked on an affair with the young man that would ruin her career and take her country's politics to the brink.

Her extraordinary summer of love was complicated by her husband, Peter Robinson, simultaneously becoming Northern Ireland's first minister in June 2008, making them the country's most prominent, glamorous power couple. Where he was the quiet man following in the noisier footsteps of the puritanical preacher and former DUP leader Rev. Ian Paisley, she was the good-time glamorous granny, with the wind in her dyed hair as she charged around the country with the top down on her latest luxury convertible. The couple became known as 'Swish Family Robinson', having drawn on so many taxpayer-funded expenses and salaries. At their Belfast home they boasted of a huge four-poster Gothic bed with heart-shaped cushions, a fresco of the Tuscan countryside over the bath and a chandelier in every room.

Yet the conspicuous largesse of this political Posh and Becks sat uneasily alongside their fire-and-brimstone pronouncements. Iris, a fundamentalist member of the evangelical Free Methodist Church, unfathomably chose the day Peter took office as first minister to go on the BBC and call homosexuality 'an abomination'. A couple of weeks later she declared: 'There can be no viler act, apart from homosexuality and sodomy, than sexually abusing innocent children.' Quite where adultery sat on her warped league table of sin was not made clear.

Around the same time, Castlereagh borough council, on which Iris was a councillor, advertised for someone to run a café which it had built on the banks of the River Lagan. Iris was thrilled when her secret lover, Kirk, was the only person who met all the criteria, and not just because of her romantic interest – she had a financial interest too. Unbeknown to the council, she had enlisted the help of two property developers to hand over £50,000 to fund the café project, and then she asked Kirk for £5,000 in cash as a kickback for sorting out the deal. On 28 August 2008 the council agreed to the tenancy, and Kirk signed the lease on the Lock Keeper's Inn café, ready to start serving cooked breakfasts, paninis and frothy coffees.

'We knew there would be a desire for people to enjoy small simple pleasures in their otherwise hectic lives,' Kirk said at the time. 'And that's what they find in the Lock Keeper's Inn.' Except the small simple pleasures of having an affair with a married woman twice his age took their toll.

After Iris bombarded him with emails, texts and love letters, Kirk – who also had a teenage girlfriend at the time – took drastic action. He told her he had testicular cancer that threatened his life and affected his sexual performance, the *Irish Independent* reported. For whatever reason, they split. Iris texted her friend Selwyn Black, who would eventually go public with the whole saga, explaining the relationship was off: 'Just cut links with Kirk. God's word was very clear on it. He was reasonably OK on it. I am not.' Bit late to be worrying about God, you might think. Anyway, then she set about trying to get her money back. 'It seems cruel but I am not going to soften until he has paid back the 45k and he has got until Christmas,' she texted Black. 'Everything is a reminder wherever I go. My home, my church, my car, my music and of course the roads we drove.' She chops and changes a bit on whether the money was going to go back to the developers or was to be split with her local church.

In March 2009 Peter found out about his wife's affair with the young man from the café. In a night of high personal drama, Iris attempted to take her own life. Hours later Peter went to work at Stormont and was seen joking with colleagues. He thinks about leaving her, but decides to keep quiet about the whole business and continue as first minister.

Then, apparently out of nowhere, in January 2010 tearful press statements were hastily arranged so that Peter could go public on the affair, even the suicide attempt and why he stood by her: 'I determined that I could not walk away without making a genuine effort to see if my marriage could be saved. That is the road I am on.' And Iris insisted it all meant nothing: 'It had no emotional or lasting meaning but my actions have devastated my life and the lives of those around me.'

Why the sudden rush to public confession? The next day a BBC *Spotlight* investigation revealed details of the texts sent to Black, the affair and the £50,000 for the café. Shell-shocked, Peter stepped down as first minister temporarily, handing over to Arlene Foster. People in Northern Ireland, who had spent years being judged by perhaps the most sanctimonious people in public life, revelled in the revelation that the Robinsons were as fallible as the rest of them.

All of which Hillary Clinton was mulling as she read the memo marked 'Northern Ireland crisis'. In it Blumenthal explained that the future of further devolution to Northern Ireland was in jeopardy. Peter was 'incapable of acting' and the DUP was left 'in suspended animation', while 'the silence of Sinn Fein is telling'. Shaun Woodward, the Northern Ireland secretary, had warned that if Peter resigned an Assembly election would have to be called 'in which they would be tainted by him and suffer a catastrophic defeat'.

A general election due months later would make matters worse. Woodward was said to be pushing the DUP 'not to scuttle the peace process but to embrace it and move forward', while also working through the Irish government to communicate to Sinn Fein's Gerry Adams 'not to provoke a full-blown crisis, ruining peace prospects in order to advance the dream of a united Ireland'. The memo suggested that Peter's six-week hiatus 'puts the DUP in a fugue state, a twilight zone of disorientation, that cannot be sustained even this week'.

Yet, amazingly, sustain it did. After his six-week break Peter returned to his job. Iris, by contrast, quit all three political jobs soon after the scandal broke, and in 2014 was found to have broken Assembly rules by failing to declare cash payments. Peter was cleared of wrongdoing and remained as first minister until 11 January 2016, exactly six years to the day from when the scandal first broke. On the day he quit, 5,000 miles away dancing on *The Ellen DeGeneres Show* was Hillary Clinton, a woman who knows a thing or two about being the innocent spouse in a political sex affair.

# 37

# Nick Griffin's kitchen, Welshpool

*Sunday, 22 December 2013*

Swedes. It's a winter's afternoon and Nick Griffin, leader of the far-right British National Party, is railing against them. You might think it makes a change from attacking other nationalities, except this time he is focusing his ire on vegetables. 'You can have too much swede,' he declares. 'Unless you are a goat.' Turning his attention to carrots, wielding a huge knife with the confidence of a man who doesn't have only one eye, he lops off the end before suggesting 'you could eat that bit if you're really hard up or skint'.

This is cooking on a budget with Nick Griffin. Or, as he put it, a 'recipe for beating the Tory blues'. In a very strange video that lasts a YouTube-unfriendly thirty-three minutes but actually feels even longer, Griffin swigs beer like a pound-shop Keith Floyd while imparting such culinary wisdom as not eating the skin of an onion and why supermarket ready meals are 'not fit for animals to eat'.

In his Montgomeryshire home on the England/Wales border he is demonstrating how easy it is to make a patriotic Great British Stew, using discounted beef, onions, carrots, beer, tabasco and, yes, swede. In a Help for Heroes rugby shirt, he ducks under the low beams as he goes on and on and on about the merits of cheap meat. He tells viewers: 'One of our chaps in Birmingham was saying that people he works with were saying they simply cannot afford, their wives cannot afford to put enough decent food on the table.' Finally, someone is thinking of the right-wing chaps who can't even have a decent meal waiting for them on the table when they get home to the cash-strapped wife after a long day rabble-rousing. The video, uploaded on 22 December 2013, has been watched 100,000 times in the past decade.

Griffin is wearing a big watch, but doesn't need to look at it because there is a huge faux antique timepiece hanging over the Aga, purchased presumably because he misheard people shouting 'massive clock' at him in the street. Ironically, at one point he says: 'The only reason for not cooking is if you haven't got the time.'

Yet by Christmas 2013, time was something that Griffin had increasingly in abundance. Having topped out their support in the early Noughties, by then the BNP had been on the wane for years. Media appearances, most notably on *Question Time* in 2009, fuelled electoral gains, which saw the party peak at fifty councillors and Griffin himself become one of two BNP members of the European Parliament. But these were slowly reversed by spirited local campaigns.

In May 2014, Griffin appeared on Sky News with some more culinary (and racist) news, boasting that he was going to open a whites-only food bank. 'Yep we are indeed what you call racist,' he declared with a chuckle. But the voters had just had the last laugh. The BNP had lost all their seats in the European Parliament elections. Within months Griffin, having already been declared bankrupt, would be kicked out of the BNP. In the 2019 general election the BNP won just 510 votes, down from more than half a million in 2010. Whatever Griffin has been cooking up since, the public have found it hard to stomach.

# 38

# Costa, Milton Keynes train station

*Friday, 8 July 2016*

Alarm bells were ringing from the start. Unfortunately they were in Costa's smoke detectors, not Andrea Leadsom's head. The woman on the verge of being prime minister had agreed to give an interview to Rachel Sylvester, one half of *The Times*' regular interviewing duo with Alice Thomson that David Cameron called the 'terrible twins'. This time Sylvester was alone. More unwisely, Leadsom was too. 'I was absolutely shattered, and very reluctant to do it,' she says. 'But I'd been persuaded that this was going to be a soft, fluffy get-to-know-you.' Instead, what unfolded in the coffee shop at Milton Keynes train station would help to end her run to replace Cameron, who had resigned after losing his EU referendum a fortnight earlier.

It wasn't even supposed to be there. The interview was originally planned for London, but a diary mix-up meant it was shifted to Leadsom's South Northamptonshire constituency. And the station coffee shop was the nearest venue. After kissing goodbye to her husband Ben, Leadsom was alone with Sylvester. Any senior (and plenty of not remotely senior) politicians giving an interview would have an aide with them, and they would make a recording of the conversation in case of a discrepancy later.

Leadsom had neither. 'It was ridiculous to not take anyone else along, and to not even record it,' she says more than six years later. 'It was just a lack of experience. And then of course the awful thing was . . . I mean, it was very sweet, actually, but all these other coffee drinkers kept coming over saying, "Hello, are you Andrea Leadsom? I voted for you. I voted Leave. It's fantastic to see you here." And I'm like, "Thank you so much but I'm just doing an interview." It was unbelievable. You could do a very funny sketch about it. It took me a long time to laugh about it, I must say.'

At the time of the *Times* interview she had been an MP for six years and a middle-ranking minister for just over two. By contrast Theresa May, her rival to be PM, had been an MP for nineteen years, and home secretary for six. No wonder Leadsom had found the early skirmishes of the leadership contest bruising and exhausting. In Costa she began to cry when recalling her mother coping after divorcing her father, and Sylvester remembers her being 'brittle and quite overwhelmed by the whole experience'. She seemed to lose the plot when answering *The Times*'s traditional, jokey quickfire questions. Asked 'Continuity or change?', she replied 'Both.' She said the same when asked to choose between hugging huskies or hunting with hounds. Leopard-skin kitten heels or ballet pumps? Leadsom fumed: 'I hate that question.' Pressed to pick between Jamie Oliver and Delia Smith, she snapped: 'I'm not answering any more. These are divisive questions.'

More consequentially, in the main interview Sylvester asked Leadsom how she was different from her rival. 'I see myself as one, an optimist, and two, a member of a huge family and that's important to me,' Leadsom replied. 'My kids are a huge part of my life.' May, by contrast, had spoken only a week earlier about her sadness about not having been able to have children with husband Philip: 'Sometimes things you wish had happened don't, or there are things you wish you'd been able to do, but can't.'

Sylvester noted that Leadsom had repeatedly referred to being a mum during her pro-Brexit referendum campaign appearances, and asked if she 'feels like a mum in politics'. 'Yes,' Leadsom replied, and warmed to her theme: 'I don't really know Theresa very well but I am sure she will be really, really sad that she doesn't have children so I don't want this to be "Andrea has children, Theresa hasn't," because I think that would be really horrible but genuinely I feel being a mum means you have a very real stake in the future of our country, a tangible stake. She possibly has nieces, nephews, lots of people, but I have children who are going to have children who will directly be a part of what happens next. So it really keeps you focused on what are you really saying.'

At 10.01 p.m. on Friday, *The Times*'s front page appeared online with the headline 'Being a mother gives me edge on May – Leadsom'. She was furious, tweeting first at 10.41 p.m.: 'Truly appalling, and the exact opposite of what I said. I am disgusted.' And then at 10.55 p.m.: 'This is despicable and hateful reporting. You must now provide the transcript – this is beyond disgusting.' Then at 11.13 p.m. she tweeted at Sylvester: 'This is the worst gutter journalism I've ever seen. I am so angry – I can't believe this. How could you?' *The Times* did indeed provide the transcript, which showed that Leadsom had not said the opposite at all. Some of the audio was also released, complete with babies crying, and the fire alarm sounding in the coffee shop. It confirmed she had said it.

Leadsom says now: 'Basically what was happening was I was explaining to that journalist – who shall not be named, by me anyway – what it was that I didn't want her to write. And therefore I was sort of assuming that she wouldn't write it because I'd asked her not to. But of course, since it was an on-the-record interview, having set the terms of the interview, you don't then get to change them halfway through. And that was the problem, that is totally on me. You know, it was ridiculous, and to not take anyone else along, and to not even record it.'

Her critics seized on the episode as proof of her inexperience – 'No time for a novice' – and pressure mounted for her to pull out of the race. In fact, Leadsom says it had been on her mind for days before she even ordered her fateful coffee: 'One of the totemic moments was getting a call from a very senior civil servant in the Cabinet Office saying: "So Mrs Leadsom. If you become Prime Minister, what will be your Day One policies?" And I was like: "Oh, my gosh." You've said, "I'm going to get Brexit done," and you haven't really thought about what the rest of your manifesto might be. And you're a Conservative, and it's a Conservative government, and someone asks you that question, what do you answer?' She had been daunted from the moment she heard that she was in the final two of what was a chaotic and volatile leadership contest: frontrunner Boris Johnson pulled out after losing the support of his Vote Leave wingman Michael Gove, who then ran himself; Stephen Crabb, who came fourth, would be revealed, on the same *Times* front page as the Leadsom 'mother' interview, to be a serial sexter of a young woman who was not his wife.

In the first ballot of Conservative MPs, May had secured an impressive 50 per cent of the vote even when there were four other candidates in the race. In the second ballot she got 60.5 per cent, ahead of Leadsom on 25.5 per cent, and Gove trailing on 14 per cent, who was then eliminated. Leadsom had been alarmed to discover that a nine-week contest wooing the party members would follow, in part because Cameron was keen on a long goodbye tour which would take in a G20 summit in China. 'I said "we can't have a nine-week campaign – sterling's dropping, the stock markets are jittering, we can't possibly do that to the country". All of those things conspired to make me think, well, actually, if we can't have a short campaign, it's just not in the country's interest for me to carry on regardless, when really the weight of support was with Theresa.'

So just after midday on Monday, 11 July, barely seventy-two hours after that Costa coffee, she stood on the steps of her campaign HQ and announced: 'I have concluded that the interests of our country are best served by the immediate appointment of a strong and well-supported prime minister. I am therefore withdrawing from the leadership election and I wish Theresa May the very greatest success.' While this was unfolding, I was heading back to London after seeing Cameron make what turned out to be his last public speech at the Farnborough Airshow. The alert came through while I was in a coffee shop at Farnborough train station. I had nobody with me to record the moment. But then I wasn't running to be prime minister.

# 39

# Co-op, The Strand

*Friday, 16 April 2021*

'Is everything all right here?' It's a good question. I'm clutching a bottle of wine in each hand and the shop assistant is wondering why I'm not using a basket like a normal person. 'I am going to pay for it, don't worry,' I tell him. 'OK,' he says, not entirely convinced. 'I'm not going to run off.' 'OK.' 'I promise.' 'OK.' 'I just want to see how much I can fit in a suitcase.' It turns out that you can comfortably get eight bottles of very agreeable wine (six white, two red) in a hand luggage-sized wheelie case, although with a bit of planning and more padding to stop the clanking of glass you could probably pack in ten, maybe even twelve.

If I was more practised at it, I would have known to not pack the wine carefully into the case before paying, because after zipping it up and wheeling it to the till you then need to bend over, unzip it and empty it all again, slowing down the whole process. In all it took me five minutes from entering the Co-op, walking past the fruit juice, and sandwiches, and chocolate and the bread aisle, right to the back of the store, loading up the case, emptying the case, paying the £71 charge at the till, reloading the case and getting back onto the Strand. You could do it faster with practice, of which Number 10 staff have had plenty over the years.

In the Middle Ages, what is now Downing Street was the site of the Axe brewery, owned by the Abbey of Abingdon. Fast forward about half a millennium, and the booze was flowing on the same spot. On Friday, 16 April 2021 there were two leaving dos in Number 10: one for James Slack, the former *Daily Mail* journalist who had been director of communications since the departure of Lee Cain, who had left along with his ally Dominic Cummings five months earlier. The other leaving party was for one of Johnson's personal photographers. At the time England was in Step Two of Covid rules on socialising, and gatherings of two or more people indoors were banned, as were groups of more than six outdoors, 'subject to exceptions which included where a gathering was reasonably necessary . . . for work purposes'.

An invite for Slack's bash had been sent to more than seventy-seven members of staff a couple of weeks in advance. Around forty-five people turned up, drank booze and ate food. It began at around 6.30 p.m. with speeches from Slack and his successor as the PM's spokesman Max Blain, with some watching on Zoom from home. Incredibly, given the fact that many present were later fined for breaking the lockdown rules they helped write, one of the official Number 10 photographers came in to record the illegal occasion for posterity. The pictures, which were later shared in WhatsApp groups, show gaggles of people drinking. The revelry went on for several hours, even after some staff had gone back to work or gone home. The stragglers were told to leave by the Downing Street custodians who look after the place and were trying to lock up, so they went into the Number 10 garden.

The other event had been organised on the day, and was held in the basement where the digital team was based. It began at about the same time as Slack's, with about fifteen to twenty people present. Someone set up a laptop on a printer to play music. Shelley Williams-Walker, Johnson's head of operations, was the evening's DJ. She was previously best known as the Johnson aide who grabbed a coffee out of his hands on camera, telling her supposedly green boss: 'No disposable cups.' No such concern while she was spinning the platters that matter for her colleagues. 'Several people were properly pissed,' said one person present. 'It was a mess.' There was concern about the amount of wine being sloshed onto the carpet, so they too ventured out into the garden, apparently confident that the high red-brick wall shielded them from prying eyes.

It became clear that they were running out of booze, so someone grabbed the suitcase kept in the press office for years for precisely this purpose and made the eight-minute walk to the Co-op on the Strand to stock up on more drink. None of this was a one-off. In December 2020 staff had a whip-round to raise £200 to buy a wine fridge to be installed in the Downing Street press office. Chilling up to thirty-four bottles at 5 degrees C, it fuelled what were regular 'wine-time Fridays'. By 9.30 p.m. that Friday there were more than twenty people outside drinking. Some started playing with the toys belonging to Wilf, son of Boris and Carrie Johnson. They went on the swing and broke it. If someone didn't say, 'Next slide please' they have no business running the country. As it got dark and turned colder the group broke up and some drifted home, but a hardcore went back into Downing Street and continued drinking. Exit logs handed over to the Sue Gray inquiry into lockdown parties showed that some left after midnight, others between 1.45 and 2.45 a.m. Two members of staff stayed later still, with one leaving at 3.11 a.m. and the last leaving at 4.20 a.m.

All of which means there were more people at the leaving dos on that Friday night than could attend the funeral of Prince Philip the next day, when Covid restrictions, drawn up in Downing Street, capped mourner numbers at thirty. In one of the most iconic images from an iconic life, Queen Elizabeth was forced to sit utterly alone, wearing a black facemask, in St George's Chapel at Windsor Castle while the Number 10 kids were nursing their hangovers. If Downing Street staff had turned up for work that Saturday morning they would have seen the Union flag flying at half-mast over Number 10 in tribute to the Duke of Edinburgh. Slack, who went on to become deputy editor of *The Sun*, later apologised, saying the event 'should not have happened at the time that it did'.

Johnson was not there that night, though it is hard to argue that the culture of the place isn't set by the top. More than once he denied any wrongdoing, saying that 'All guidance was followed completely in Number 10' and 'I have been repeatedly assured since these allegations emerged that there was no party and that no Covid rules were broken.' These claims triggered a privileges committee investigation over whether he had misled parliament. His supporters maintained that all the revelry in Number 10 was fine because these people were spending hours together anyway; so if they were sitting in meetings drawing up legislation by day, there was no extra harm if they downed a load of Peronis and touched each other up in the kitchens by night.

The police disagreed, and in the end 126 fines were issued – fifty-three to men and seventy-three to women – including twenty-eight people who were fined more than once. They related to eight different dates, including the wine suitcase night on 16 April 2021, the last of the rule-breaking bashes. There was also 20 May 2020, 18 June 2020, 19 June 2020, 13 November 2020, 17 December 2020, 18 December 2020 and 14 January 2021. It's hard to read a list of dates like that without glazing over. It is why memorable details matter. Along with photographs of Johnson toasting colleagues surrounded by bottles, and the absurd claim that the PM had been "ambushed with a cake" on his birthday, the suitcase of booze became an unforgettable symbol of everything that was wrong with what went on inside Downing Street while the rest of the country was holed up at home, raising a toast over Zoom to departing colleagues and departed loved ones.

Having a suitcase to hand suggests premeditation. Knowing not to go to the much closer Tesco at Westminster station but the very slightly further afield Co-op hints at illicitness. As does arriving with your swag through the back gates of Downing Street. A suitcase of booze screams pre-planned piss-up. It's why public anger erupted in the way it did. In November 2021, before the partygate story first broke, 43 per cent of the public thought Johnson was likeable. But three months later YouGov's tracker found that it had fallen to just 32 per cent, which is kryptonite for a man whose entire career has been based on personal appeal over policy detail or even political nous. More than half disliked him, two-thirds considered him incompetent, three-quarters said he was untrustworthy.

In April 2022, less than three years after becoming prime minister, Johnson was referred to the privileges committee to consider whether he had misled the House of Commons and whether that conduct amounted to a contempt. The decision was approved unanimously without a vote while Johnson was still PM. When the next scandal broke – what Johnson did or didn't know about the behaviour of his deputy chief whip, Christopher Pincher – the benefit of the doubt was long gone, and so too was he, leaving Number 10 in July 2022.

Almost a year and two prime ministers later, amid much talk of kangaroo courts, witch-hunts and other mixed metaphors, the privileges committee concluded that Johnson had indeed knowingly misled the House, and would have faced an extraordinary ninety-day suspension from the Commons. It was an unprecedented rebuke for a former PM. Rather than face the music, Johnson had already quit as an MP and rushed for the exit, like just-fired *Apprentice* candidates trailing a wheelie case out of the building and still telling the taxi drivers this was all a terrible mistake.

*Homes*

# 40

# Tamhorn Park Farmhouse, Tamworth

*Thursday, 18 December 1834*

Manifestos are like porn mags. Everybody seems to know what is in them, but nobody would ever own up to actually reading one. And yet despite being such a neglected branch of literature, their contents can suddenly take on great, quasi-religious significance. Especially when a party enters government and starts doing things which break an apparently key manifesto pledge (which often went totally unnoticed before polling day). In 2017, just one in ten people told pollsters BMG that they 'always read manifestos', which is the same proportion of people who did not know what a manifesto was (although I suppose it's possible they had been reading them without knowing).

In politics, less is more. Boris Johnson's 2019 landslide-winning Conservative manifesto was just a thin sixty-four pages long, while Jeremy Corbyn's losing Labour effort was almost twice that at 107 pages. Quite a step up from Labour's 2017 arguably more successful, majority-denying manifesto which was forty-odd pages long. In 2015 the Lib Dems offered up 33,000 words over 160 pages, which helped them to the worst result since the party's formation.

All of them, though, were much longer than the original political manifesto: a twelve-page pamphlet published by Sir Robert
Peel, the Conservative MP for Tamworth, who kept Tamhorn
Park Farmhouse just outside the town as a hunting lodge and
rural retreat. In late 1834 Peel was invited by King William IV
to form a government as the new prime minister (the Duke of
Wellington stood in for the first fortnight because Peel was on
holiday in Rome). Peel returned from his travels and called an
election to secure his own mandate and, unlike any British party
leader before him, he chose to write down those plans.

Peel had already cemented his place in history as a great
reforming home secretary, founding what is now the Metropoli-
tan Police, with officers known as Peelers or Bobbies in his
honour. Now the country was still adjusting to the riotous passing of the Great Reform Act two years earlier – sweeping away
the rotten boroughs with few voters and increasing the electorate
by around three-quarters to 600,000. Far from full democracy,
but a lot closer than it had ever been.

'I feel it incumbent upon me to enter into a full declaration of
my views on public policy, as full and unreserved as I can make
it,' Peel's Tamworth manifesto began. He had opposed the Great
Reform Act, but now wanted to make it clear that he accepted it.
No going back. It was, he wrote, 'a final and irrevocable settlement of a great constitutional question – a settlement which no
friend to the peace and welfare of this country would attempt to
disturb, either by direct or by insidious means'.

He would abide by the spirit of the Act if it only meant 'a careful review of institutions, civil and ecclesiastical, undertaken in a
friendly temper, combining, with the firm maintenance of estab-
lished rights, the correction of proved abuses, and the redress of
real grievances'. He would not, though, go along with anything
which 'meant we are to live in a perpetual vortex of agitation'. In
other words, the Conservatives would embrace past modest
reform in order to preserve institutions in future. This was the
essence of Conservatism, and remained so for decades. (Arguably,

one of the biggest anomalies with Brexit was that it was so, well, un-Conservative: throwing everything up in the air in a fit of radical pique rather than pursuing change incrementally.)

In his Tamworth manifesto Peel also railed against 'vague and unmeaning professions of popular opinion' from politicians who then failed to stick to them. Well, there have been plenty of those since. Johnson's 2019 manifesto promised: 'We will not raise the rate of income tax, VAT or National Insurance', before moving to increase National Insurance to raise billions for the NHS and social care – a U-turn which was then U-turned upon by Liz Truss during her brief premiership and stuck to by Rishi Sunak. Theresa May has the rare honour of U-turning on a manifesto pledge even before a single vote had been cast, again on the thorny issue of funding social care. In 2017 her manifesto pledged to increase to £100,000 the amount someone could hold in assets before having to pay for care. After that people who had 'built considerable property assets due to rising property prices' would have to stump up. Tory MPs reported a furious backlash on the doorstep. Launched on 18 May, a reversal was performed four days later, promising 'an absolute limit' or cap on care costs. Bizarrely, May appeared to be in denial about the reversal, declaring: 'Nothing has changed, nothing has changed.' Something did change: a fortnight later she lost her majority. Grant Shapps, the Tory cabinet minister, later described it as the 'world's worst manifesto from the world's oldest political party'.

Providing some competition for the worst manifesto is Labour's 1983 offering. Michael Foot's socialist prospectus, *The New Hope for Britain*, promised across thirty-nine pages unilateral nuclear disarmament, renationalisation of heavy industry, departure from the EEC, abolition of the House of Lords and increased taxes on the wealthy. The Labour MP Gerald Kaufman called it the 'longest suicide note in history' after the party lost 60 seats, handing Margaret Thatcher a landslide majority of 144.

Perhaps the biggest, and most consequential, broken manifesto pledge in recent times were the twenty-one words in the Lib

Dems' prospectus in 2010: 'We will scrap unfair university tuition fees so everyone has the chance to get a degree, regardless of their parents' income.' What they did was ever so slightly different. In coalition with the Conservatives, they saw tuition fees treble to £9,000 a year. And the Lib Dems were almost wiped out five years later. Not that shredding a manifesto promise is always terminal. In 1997 Tony Blair promised that New Labour 'has no plans to introduce tuition fees for higher education', before moving to do just that after two months in power. He went on to win two more elections.

No such luck for Peel – in the January 1835 election his Conservatives were trounced by the Whigs by 385 seats to 273. He finally won an election in 1841, and five years later sought to repeal the Corn Laws, which were keeping food prices artificially high while Ireland was in the grip of famine. He arguably did the right thing by the country, but lost the support of two-thirds of his own party. In the election that followed, the party was turfed out by voters. No manifesto could save him this time.

# 41

# The Hillocks, Lossiemouth

*Christmas 1923*

Ramsay MacDonald had a miserable Christmas. Being back home in his beloved 'Lossie' only deepened his grief for his wife, Margaret, who had been dead for eleven years, and for his son David, dead for one year more. To make matters worse, this maudlin single father of five was about to become prime minister.

MacDonald's story is incredible, the sort of tale that might make the most audacious scriptwriter blush. The illegitimate child of a housemaid and a farm labourer – whom he only saw once in his life when his mother took him to the top of a hill and pointed out the distant ploughman in the valley below – he travelled a long way geographically, socially and politically to become the first ever Labour prime minister, only for his party to later disown him as a traitor and write him out of its collective history. Yet it is a story that is now mostly forgotten or overlooked because it played out just before the Second World War and most modern politics seems to begin with Churchill and all of that. Even the least successful American president has their own library, but I soon discovered that the collected works of one of our most groundbreaking prime ministers are confined to a beige cardboard box seldom summoned from the National Archives. In these diaries he confessed his hopes, fears, private triumphs and grief, putting his feelings down on the page because there was no one else to share them with.

MacDonald was an early Labour MP from 1906 to 1918, when he lost his seat in Leicester having been an outspoken opponent of British involvement in the First World War. He was ostracised by some of his colleagues for his pacifism, and Moray golf club in Lossiemouth, where he enjoyed playing, banned him for endangering the 'character and interests of the club'. In 1922 he was elected again as a Labour MP, this time for Aberavon in South Wales, and within a week he challenged the incumbent chairman of the Labour Party, J. R. Clynes, over his leadership. This was despite Labour having just gained dozens of seats in the general election to become the second-largest party behind Bonar Law's Conservatives. Against MacDonald's own expectations he won, becoming the first person to be known officially as leader of the Labour Party. He was immediately frustrated by his colleagues, who he felt had no sense of parliamentary tactics. He was also lonely, unable to share his success with his wife. 'All my people are dead,' he wrote in his diary. 'The victory has come when there is no one to cheer.'

In May 1923 ill-health forced Bonar Law to resign, and Stanley Baldwin became Conservative prime minister, inheriting a majority of more than 70. But he wanted to change government policy on trade, introducing protectionist tariffs on imports, and quaintly felt he should hold a general election, even though he didn't need to. He quickly wished he hadn't. On 6 December 1923 the Conservatives lost 86 seats, to be left with 258, some 50 short of a majority. Labour, led by the dashing MacDonald with his white hair and dark moustache, were up 49 on 191 seats, while Asquith's Liberals were up 43 on 158. A hung parliament, then, without a clear winner, but a clear loser: Baldwin.

In the days after the election, the evening papers were full of talk about how Baldwin would resign within days and King George V would send for MacDonald to become Labour's first prime minister. Again he lamented being unable to share it with Margaret. 'Were she here to help me. Why are they both dead – my mother and she.' In fact it would all take a little while longer, with some Labour colleagues advising him not to even think about entering government. It made him realise that a party that had grown quickly from just two MPs at the turn of the century to the brink of power might struggle to rise to the occasion.

A national debate erupted over parliamentary arithmetic, and whether staid old Britain was really ready for a radical Labour government. Winston Churchill, who had just lost his seat as a Liberal, called the idea a 'national misfortune'. George Terrell, a Conservative MP who had also just been ousted, wrote to *The Times* that Labour was supported by 'Communists, the wild men, the work-shy, the ignorant, the illiterate' and warned that a 'bull in a china-shop would be a child' compared to a Labour chancellor in the Treasury, adding: 'We simply cannot afford this experiment.' Some thought the Conservatives should prop up the Liberals, others vice versa. Asquith made it clear that his Liberal Party could not keep the Conservatives in power, and suggested that a Labour government 'could hardly be tried under safer conditions'. The nation would spend Christmas debating the issue.

On Saturday, 15 December MacDonald travelled home to Lossiemouth to consider his options. In a sign that life was changing, his usual quiet arrival was replaced by large waiting crowds, the town's local fishermen and their families turning out to cheer the man of the moment, with the whistles of trains and even the sirens of boats out at sea joining in the cacophony. He returned to The Hillocks, the house he built in 1910 for his mother and where he lived for most of his life. His granddaughter, Iona Kielhorn, still lives in in the house, and tells me how he had originally wanted to build it on the smarter Prospect Terrace at the top of a hill to enjoy what he considered the best view in the world, but was told: 'Red bastards do not build up here.' He was sent to the Seatown 'slum' area of Lossiemouth instead. From the road the house does not look much, with just two windows breaking up the vast grey-stone wall. But the front of the house looks out over the garden, with two large bay windows and a veranda from where he could sit and contemplate his political fate.

It was here that he began considering who might be in his cabinet, even whether they had enough good people to reassure the voters, the bankers and the Army that a Labour government could be trusted. He was trying to balance trade unionists and those with government experience, ensuring the inclusion of names from both the left and right of the party, describing cabinet-making as 'the most horrible job in my life'. At his desk he could look out of one window to the golden sands and icy water of Lossiemouth's east beach, while out of another window to the west he could see the Scottish Highlands. He would work late by the light of a green-shaded oil lamp, and recalled how he 'spent Christmas and New Year immersed in politics, and loads of letters at Lossiemouth'. In 1923 The Hillocks had no telephone; one would have to be installed so Downing Street could contact him. Those letters included writing to Arthur Henderson, his deputy, who lost his seat in the election and for whom he did not have a high regard. 'I have tried a list of Ministers without you, and with you as Chairman of Ways and Means.' It was a snub. Chairman of Ways and Means is not even a government job, and it caused a huge row. Henderson would eventually be found a seat and become home secretary, with Philip Snowden as an orthodox, don't-startle-the-horses chancellor, and MacDonald himself taking foreign secretary as well as PM.

He was not a great diarist, suffering from a relatable complaint that when significant events worth recording occurred he was too busy to record them. Lifting the tatty, thick, dark-blue leatherbound journal out of a box at the National Archives, the first thing I find is a handwritten note on the inside cover making it clear that it was only to 'guide and revive memory' and was never to be published in full. The diaries do, however, reveal a lonely man contemplating taking on the loneliest job. 'Times of sad reflections and gloomy thoughts. The people of my heart are dead; their faces on my walls, they do not share with me. Had much difficulty in returning. How vain is honour now. My dearest living friends cannot change my heart from a grave & myself from being a solitary.' He was not entirely alone, though. To the consternation of his diehard Labour colleagues, he took advice from more recent converts to the socialist cause. He was visited in Lossie by General C. B. Thomson, who was more golf partner than political strategist, but would go on to be given a peerage in order to become the secretary of state for air. They would often be seen yomping around the Scottish countryside, and the golf course at Spey.

Having resolved to try to form a government, and sketched out the names who might fill it, it was time to leave for London. The people of Lossie had been kind to him, 'but I have to work out my destiny. So I returned to the world of politics & premierships, & a press that wonders why I take so little delight in publicity.' On 8 January 1924 Labour held a victory rally in a packed Royal Albert Hall at which MacDonald was cheered, while cautioning his colleagues against premature triumphalism. The singing of socialist anthems 'The Red Flag' and 'La Marseillaise' raised eyebrows, including at Buckingham Palace.

The process of filling every ministerial office continued. There were no Labour peers, so some would have to be created to take key jobs. MacDonald was dismayed by the whole process: only a couple of his colleagues were grateful just to be offered a job, with one after another behaving as if the offer of ministerial office was an insult. One aggrieved colleague had his wife write to MacDonald to complain. 'I feel like an executioner,' MacDonald wrote in his diary, 'I knock so many ambitious heads into my basket. After this every man will be my enemy.' It is a sentiment with which every reshuffling prime minister since would no doubt sympathise.

As the moment of truth grew closer, he remained strangely detached. He was sent details of the procedure for him to visit

Buckingham Palace and be invited to form a government, yet it all remained illusory. 'I sometimes feel I should like to run away to Lossie to return to reality and flee from these unreal dreams.' He was torn between his socialist roots and love of the simple life, and his belief in Parliament to change things.

On 21 January Baldwin's outgoing government was defeated in a confidence vote in the Commons, and it was official: MacDonald would become the first Labour prime minister. 'The load will be heavy, and I am so much alone.' Yet he was surrounded by his colleagues in the ensuing days as they marched off to Buckingham Palace, most (if not all) in ceremonial dress: socialists going down on bended knee to the monarch. It was a unique moment, when a political party which had not existed twenty years before had risen up from working-class union movements to take control of the nation, peacefully too. 'Without fuss, the firing of guns, the flying of new flags, the Labour government has come,' MacDonald wrote of the occasion in his diary. The king recorded it too: 'Today 23 years ago dear Grandma died. I wonder what she would have made of a Labour Government.'

Whatever she would have made of it, it would not last long. In October 1924 the Liberals lost patience and voted the Labour government out. It would be another five years before MacDonald would return as prime minister, after Labour won the most seats in the 1929 election. While able to bring about some change domestically, including tackling unemployment benefits and slum housing, when the Great Depression hit his party was split on how to respond, with some ministers threatening to quit if there were government spending cuts. MacDonald's own resignation was rejected by George V, who instead urged him to form a National Government with the Liberals and Conservatives, which he did. For his trouble MacDonald was thrown out of the Labour Party, but remained prime minister. At the 1931 election the National Government won 554 seats, but included only 13 for MacDonald's National Labour. Always a sensitive man, he was deeply hurt by the rejection of the movement he helped to found and forge into a party of government, but he remained in office until ill-health forced his retirement in 1935. Throughout that time he was supported by his eldest daughter, Ishbel, who would play the role of consort and hostess in Number 10. Furniture, including his desk, inkpot and alarming bear rug, would be sent from Lossiemouth, and even girls from the town would be hired to staff the place. It was all a reminder of home in Lossie, where he would always rather be.

# 42

# Abbey Road, London

*Friday, 7 August 1925*

Maundy Gregory was a happy man. He had just helped broker his biggest and best set of honours yet. And now he was celebrating by moving into Abbey Lodge, a double-fronted detached Victorian villa in a smart corner of north-west London.

He would live upstairs as the gay bachelor, while the rooms downstairs went to his old friends Fred and Edith Rosse. There would be parties, cocktails, champagne and fireworks. The gramophone would blare out ragtime records and revellers would gather round the grand piano for sing-alongs. Music would echo through the halls of 3 Abbey Road, as it would do forty years later when the Beatles would make the house their musical home, recording 190 of their 210 songs there, and famously posing on the zebra crossing outside for the cover of the album named after the famous Abbey Road studios.

All that was still to come. The summer of 1922 was a moment of triumph for Gregory, a failed actor, theatre impresario, socialite and crook. He was also likely a thief, a spy and a murderer. The son of an impoverished clergyman, he had a talent for becoming friends with, and indispensable to, the rich and powerful. He looked the part too, sporting a monocle, a ring which he claimed had once belonged to Oscar Wilde and carrying a diamond which, he claimed, was once the property of Catherine the

Great. He had set himself up with an office at 38 Parliament Street, near the Red Lion pub and just across the road from Downing Street, ostensibly running a magazine, the *Whitehall Gazette*, which gave him cover to be in and around the corridors of power.

When politicians had delicate matters to attend to, they knew whom to call. And in 1917 Lloyd George had a very delicate matter indeed. He found himself in power but without a party. With Britain three years into the First World War, he was the head of a war cabinet, backed by Conservatives and some of his Liberal colleagues. However, H. H. Asquith, who had resigned as prime minister in December 1916, remained in control of the Liberal Party, so the Lloyd George Fund was set up to bankroll his personal re-election efforts.

Behind closed doors Lloyd George would claim that selling honours was 'the cleanest way of raising money for a political party'. But he made sure he did not get his hands dirty. That job fell to Gregory.

Between 1917 and 1922 he helped Lloyd George create eighty-two new peers, most of whom were your typical band of war heroes, retired generals, ex-MPs and the like. However at least fourteen paid for their seats on the red-leather benches. Unsurprisingly, these were not upstanding members of society. As Chris Bryant details in his biography of Parliament, in June 1922 the King's birthday honours list included peerages for Sir William Vestey, a Liverpudlian meatpacker who had gone to South America to avoid taxes; Samuel Waring, a bankrupt who did not pay back his creditors despite making a fortune during the war; Sir Archibald Williamson, an oil tycoon who did business with the enemy during the war; and Sir Robert Borwick, an unremarkable custard powder mogul.

Over the years he had also helped create some 1,500 new knighthoods, and Gregory had even proposed the creation of the Order of the British Empire (OBE) for those who could not afford a full title. Cleverly Lloyd George also gave honours to the press barons of the day, making them much less keen on reporting on how others were getting their gongs. The price list was clear: £10,000 for a knighthood, £30,000 for a baronetcy, £50,000 for a seat in the House of Lords. In all around £100 million in today's money passed through Gregory's services, earning himself vast sums in commission.

That birthday honours list in 1922 went too far, though, and caused a political stink. While Gregory was settling into Abbey Road that summer, Lloyd George was feeling the heat. In the Commons on July 17, the prime minister was pressed again and again on the question of whether peerages were subject to a system of 'bargain and sale'. He responded: 'If it ever existed, it was a discreditable system. It ought never to have existed. If it does exist, it ought to be terminated, and if there were any doubt on that point, every step should be taken to deal with it.' The truth was, bluntly, that they were all at it. Bonar Law had raised tens of thousands of pounds for the Conservatives a decade earlier. Several of those honoured in Lloyd George's time were actually donors to the Unionists. And for the next decade Gregory would offer his services to whoever was willing to pay. Even the small matter of a law change did not stop him for a long time.

In the autumn of 1922 Lloyd George's fundraising was put to the test. In the election of November that year his National Liberals won only 53 seats, while Asquith's Liberals secured 62. Both were beaten by Bonar Law's Conservatives. Three years and two elections later, Stanley Baldwin was the Conservative prime minister who grasped the cash for honours nettle. In 1925 he drove through legislation which made it an offence to give or receive money 'as an inducement or reward for procuring or assisting or endeavouring to procure the grant of a dignity or title of honour to any person'.

It was a less happy day in Abbey Road when, on Friday, 7 August 1925, the Honours (Prevention of Abuses) Act became law. Undeterred, Gregory had by this point diversified into selling papal honours for the Catholic Church, and in 1928, three years after the law had changed, asked the businessman Sir George Lawson-Johnston if he would make a donation to the Conservatives in exchange for an honour. He reported it to two officials in the party, who thought they might secure the first prosecution under the new law. That was until they were told that Leigh Maclachlan, the Conservatives' principal agent, had been working with Gregory on selling knighthoods. Gregory had taken £11,000 for his troubles. The Lawson-Johnston case was quietly dropped.

Not long afterwards, Gregory and Edith Rosse (she and Fred were now estranged) left Abbey Road for 10 Hyde Park Terrace, an even smarter address which allowed Gregory to accurately interrupt meetings saying he had to take a 'call from Number 10', allowing guests to inaccurately think the PM was on the phone. And still he kept on selling honours.

In December 1932 Gregory had an associate. J. D. Moffat approach Lieutenant-Commander Edward Whaley Billyard-Leake, offering a knighthood. Over the course of several meetings and calls, Gregory said that 'sinews' would be needed to open closed doors to make it happen. It could be done for £10,000, but £12,000 would smooth the path more easily. As Andrew Cook describes in his book *Cash for Honours*, Billyard-Leake took it to the authorities, enlisting the Treasury solicitor Sir Maurice Gwyer, who listened in to the call, eyebrows aloft, while among the things Gregory also offered was a meeting with the King of Greece. When Billyard-Leake called again to say he would not proceed with the knighthood deal, with a policeman on the line too, Gregory said it was regrettable, adding: 'Couldn't you give say two or three thousand on account, to keep the pot boiling?'

Chief Inspector Arthur Askew and Detective Sergeant Gillen knocked on the not insubstantial door of 10 Hyde Park Terrace on the evening of Friday, 3 February 1933 and waited. They would be kept waiting for some time before being allowed in, and longer still before Gregory finally appeared. He was handed the summons, confirming he was being charged with trying to sell an honour to Billyard-Leake for £10,000. He was to appear in court thirteen days later. He would spend that time visiting recipients of some of his most lucrative honours seeking their financial assistance to ensure that nothing 'came out' during his little legal difficulties.

The Conservative Party panicked, with Baldwin himself urging Gregory to flee the country. By now it was too late. His passport had been surrendered. In court Chief Inspector Askew confirmed that there had been other complaints relating to 'similar transactions' involving Gregory and honours. Norman Birkett, Gregory's defence lawyer, insisted there was no need to go into all that, and actually a fine and costs would be punishment enough.

The Bow Street magistrates disagreed. After Gregory changed his plea to guilty to avoid any further revelations in court, Sir Rollo Frederick Graham-Campbell said the maximum fine of £50 would be 'wholly inadequate', but as it was the first case brought under the new law, the maximum prison sentence of three months would be too much. Gregory was therefore sentenced to serve two months in Wormwood Scrubs, and pay a fine of £50 plus 50 guineas costs.

A century since it was passed, he remains the only person to be charged under the Honours (Prevention of Abuses) Act. That's not to suggest the issue of honours has not been without controversy: from Harold Wilson's Lavender List of resignation honours for wealthy businessmen to Tony Blair being interviewed as a witness by police as part of a cash-for-honours inquiry that came to nothing. In the first two decades of this century all sixteen of the Conservative Party's main treasurers were granted peerages, before Boris Johnson used his resignation honours list to ennoble Ross Kempsell, his 31-year-old press officer who once interviewed him about painting buses, and Charlotte Owens, a junior aide who at 29 is the youngest ever life peer.

It is quite remarkable that selling honours is the thing that Gregory is perhaps best known for, given everything else of which he is accused. Victor Grayson, a socialist MP, was on to Gregory years earlier. 'This sale of honours is a national scandal,' he said in 1919. 'It can be traced right down to 10 Downing Street, and to a monocled dandy with offices in Whitehall. I know this man, and one day I will name him.' The following year Grayson disappeared. In 1970 Donald McCormick used his book *Murder by Perfection* to suggest that Grayson had been seen at Vanity Fair, a bungalow on Thames Ditton Island owned by Gregory, on the evening of Tuesday, 28 September 1920. That was the last sighting of Grayson.

Shortly afterwards Gregory moved into Vanity Fair with the Rosses, and two years later to Abbey Road and later Hyde Park Terrace. But by 1932 he had money problems. He asked Edith for help; she refused. A few days after changing her will on 15 September 1932 she died, leaving 'everything I have' to Gregory. The sum of £18,000 was not enough to clear his debts, which is why he came to offer the knighthood to Billyard-Leake.

When he was released from prison a car was waiting for him to take him to France, the Conservatives repaying their debts and buying his silence with a £2,000-a year-pension. He escaped the prospect of being arrested for Edith's murder, and enjoyed life in Paris until the Nazis arrived. He was sent to an internment camp, where he died in September 1941.

# 43

# 18 Randolph Crescent, Maida Vale

*Monday, 17 August 1936*

For a man who made his name, and fortune, being the first to accurately predict the outcome of political races, Henry Durant was always determined to come first. 'Remember that car!' he would cry, and then take his green Rover down a side street, hoping to speed round a shortcut and overtake his target, leaving his passengers suitably impressed. According to the academic Mark Roodhouse, this was standard behaviour as Durant went 'rallying into the London office' of the British Institute of Public Opinion (BIPO), which began life in his Maida Vale home.

Polling had been pioneered in America by George H. Gallup, who had been lauded for correctly forecasting that Franklin D. Roosevelt would beat Alf Landon in the 1936 US presidential election. Fiercely protective of his methods, he rejected suggestions that his polls would influence voters, insisting: 'One might as well insist that a thermometer makes the weather.'

On 17 August 1936 the *Queen Mary* arrived at Southampton, carrying among her passengers Harry Field, a Brit who had been living in the USA for two decades, returning home to find someone to run a British version of Gallup's American Institute of

Public Opinion. In search of an academic who could become a pollster, he approached the London School of Economics, who suggested six people. One of them was Henry Durant, a 34-year-old insurance clerk-turned-research student who was two years into a PhD on leisure. His wife, Ruth, was also a research student. The offer of £150 a year (£8,500 in 2023 prices) was sweetened by the fact that initially he would be able to work part-time from home at 18 Randolph Crescent.

Politics played a part too. Durant's humble upbringing as the son of a warehouseman and an office cleaner and his academic study of Marx, Engels and Trotsky fuelled his enthusiasm for socialism and social mobility. He formed the idea that polling would give voice to the silent majority of working-class Britons, claiming a social benefit to reporting what ordinary people thought. The face-to-face sample survey, where the people questioned came from specified groups in order to be representative of the country as a whole, was carried out door-to-door or even in the street. A sample of around 2,300 for a national poll was considered sufficient, although detailed breakdowns remained crude. There were also concerns about interviewers – mostly badly paid middle-aged, middle-class housewives – just making up responses to meet their quotas.

The polling began in earnest. The very first Gallup poll in Britain in January 1937 asked: 'Do you consider that the grounds of divorce should be made easier?' This was at a time when the country was gripped by the saga of twice-married Wallis Simpson seeking a divorce in order to marry Edward VIII, who had abdicated a month earlier. In the poll 58 per cent agreed that divorce should be easier, while 42 per cent disagreed. The second question asked: 'Do you consider that doctors should be given power to end the life of a person incurably ill?' Sixty-nine per cent said yes, 31 per cent said no. (In March 2023 YouGov ran a similar question: 'Should the law be changed to allow someone to assist in the suicide of someone suffering from an incurable but NOT terminal illness?' Of those who expressed a view,

55 per cent said the law should be changed.) Durant, though, always urged people reading the Gallup polls not just to concentrate on the majorities. 'History is full of examples of the minority proving right. Those who interpret polls correctly will pay at least as much attention to the small percentages as to the large.'

In early 1938 Sir Walter Layton, the editor-in-chief of the liberal-leaning *News Chronicle* owned by the Cadbury family, asked Durant to privately poll the Fulham West parliamentary by-election triggered by the death of Conservative MP Sir Cyril Cobb. It was a real test of the Gallup method. A random sample of 500 voters were interviewed, and predicted Labour would take the seat with 51.6 per cent of the vote. Labour went on to win with 52.2 per cent. Three more by-election tests – in Oxford, West Lewisham and East Norfolk – produced similar results. Layton was so impressed that in October the *News Chronicle* bought the exclusive rights to publish British Gallup polls, promising it would help to 'discover, with accuracy and without bias, what Britain thinks'.

There was some bias, though: Laurence Cadbury, chairman of the newspaper business, occasionally insisted on leading questions on conscription, Jewish refugees and rationing, which were worded to deliver results with which he agreed. The following year the BBC started using BIPO to carry out daily audience surveys, and during the Second World War the government had Durant carry out surveys into the reach of German propagandists like Lord Haw-Haw, and to monitor morale. He picked up corporate market research work with the likes of Ford, BP and Philips Electronics. While the idea of paying clients demanding extra questions was initially treated as a nuisance, he soon realised they were a way of making money. While business was doing well, his marriage wasn't, and he divorced Ruth, later marrying Margaret Collens.

The big breakthrough for political polling as we know it today came in 1945. The war meant there had been no general election for a decade, before Durant had set up BIPO. MPs had been dismissive of the idea of polling, even holding a debate at the height of the Battle of Britain, arguing about the merits of sample sizes. Winston Churchill did his best to rise above it, and the prospect of an election, telling the Commons in 1941: 'Nothing is more dangerous in war-time than to live in the temperamental atmosphere of a Gallup Poll, always feeling one's pulse and taking one's temperature.' A long way from today's poll-obsessed politicians.

A year later A. P. Herbert, an independent MP, took a swipe first at astrologers for trying to predict the end of the war, before adding: 'Going to the other end of the scale of craziness, I note that there is a thing called the "Gallup Poll". On the last occasion on which the constituents of the Gallup Poll were consulted, which was some few days ago, they were asked to say whether they thought the war could be won in 1942, in reply to which 40 per cent said "Yes", 41 per cent said "No", and 19 per cent – the glorious 19 – said "I do not know". 40 one way – 41 the other. If such are the pusillanimous vacillations of opinion among the great people, are we surprised that His Majesty's Ministers have not yet given a confident answer to the question?'

When Churchill finally went to the country in 1945, he hoped that Britain would thank him and the Conservatives for winning the war, declaring: 'We are going to win – I feel it in my bones.' He told the king as much too. Parliament was dissolved on 15 June. Ten days later Durant carried out his poll, and had the Conservatives on 41 per cent, with Clement Attlee's Labour six points ahead on 47 per cent. Uneasy about this result, even the *News Chronicle* played down its own poll, insisting it 'does not pretend to foretell the results of the election'. When the country voted on 5 July Labour won with 48 per cent, more than eight points ahead. The poll had been right.

Three decades later Durant was still playing 'I told you so', writing to *The Times*: 'During the election campaign of 1945 there was not the remotest suggestion that Attlee would win, except from an opinion poll published in one of the papers. Not even the paper itself paid any attention to polls in those days. Hence, everyone was astonished when Churchill failed to win. Today the climate of an election campaign is very different. Nobody can claim with any credibility that they are certain of victory unless they have the support of the polls. Clearly this helps to bring realism into the debate.' He went on to call the 1950, 1951 and 1955 elections correctly, doing deals later with the *Daily Express*, *Daily Mail* and *The Daily Telegraph*.

Not that polls have been perfect ever since. Many more players have entered the market since – there are twenty-two members of the British Polling Council, set up to improve the reputation of the industry by promoting transparency, if not accuracy. If the polls had been right, Remain would have won the EU referendum, although it would not have happened because Ed Miliband would have won the 2015 election for Labour, repeating Neil Kinnock's success in 1992. But after each failure the industry now has a bout of soul-searching inquests, tweaks the sampling and goes again. For all the talk about bias, pollsters only make money if they can show to clients that they call it right – and political polls are the most high-profile. As demographics and voting patterns change, so too do the polling methods. Unlike Durant's car chase, there are no shortcuts to staying ahead anymore.

# 44

# Squirrels, Kingham

*Saturday, 27 February 1960*

It started with a postcard. On an overcast Saturday morning it dropped through the letterbox of a charming thatched, seventeenth-century cottage in the Cotswolds. So began a tale of sex, blackmail and hitmen, the death of a dog, the downfall of a party leader, and, if we're being only a little foolhardy, the demise of a political class which would eventually help to sweep Margaret Thatcher to power.

The apparently innocuous card had been sent to mark the occasion of the engagement of the Queen's sister, Princess Margaret, to the photographer Antony Armstrong-Jones. The message read: 'What a pity. I rather hoped to marry one and seduce the other.' It is worth remembering that homosexuality was still very much against the law at this point. The card's author was Jeremy Thorpe MP, in public a recently elected, respectable, rising star of the Liberal Party, in reality an exhibitionist, predatory homosexual, and not too subtle about it. The recipient of the card was his friend, the Honourable Brecht Van de Vater, in public an upstanding English country gent, in reality the bankrupt son of a Welsh miner.

Thorpe was a liberal in the traditional sense, representing North Devon, deep in a region with a long attachment to the moralistic Methodist tradition. He was also a show-off, a charmer, a great mimic and wit, a cheat, a liar, a dandy, a bounder and a cad. A political ringmaster at a time when politics was still emerging from the grey cloud of the Second World War, he famously campaigned in one election on a hovercraft. He had the potential to go far.

That February morning Vater showed the postcard to one of his stable workers, Norman Josiffe, along with dozens of other letters from Thorpe, describing them oddly as his 'insurance policy'. Days later Thorpe visited Squirrels and had his fateful first meeting with Josiffe, an attractive, troubled young stable boy with whom he would become so entangled it would cost him everything. The MP gave the young man his business card, with an offer to call if he ever needed help.

Josiffe soon fell out with Vater, stole the letters as his own insurance policy, and then took Thorpe up on his offer, turning up at the Commons in November 1961 with his dog Mrs Tish, demanding help with getting his National Insurance card back from Vater, a deepening obsession which never went as far as simply applying for a new one. What followed was a tale of bleak tragedy and comic farce that no playwright would dare invent. Indeed, when it was made into a BBC drama in 2018 starring Hugh Grant and Ben Whishaw, disbelieving viewers spent much of *A Very English Scandal* googling to discover that the truth was weirder than fiction.

After their relationship blossoms, Thorpe takes Josiffe back to his own mother's house and rapes him while calling him 'Bunny', a bizarre nickname which he stupidly commits to paper in a letter promising his travel-hungry beau, 'Bunnies can (and will) go to Paris.' Things go wrong, not least in not getting a new National Insurance card, and Josiffe threatens to expose Thorpe.

By 1967 Thorpe is Liberal leader, a year later he marries, and his public star is rising. Something has to be done. That something, it turns out, is to bump off Josiffe, who by now is calling himself Norman Scott and has gone off the rails, sleeping rough, attempting suicide and now paranoid, rightly it turns out, that someone is trying to kill him. Peter Bessell, another Liberal MP, is Thorpe's self-appointed protector, tasked initially with funnelling hush money to Scott. When Bessell later leaves for America, the role is taken by David Holmes, a Liberal Party moneyman who was best man at Thorpe's wedding. Bessell claims that in late 1968 Thorpe told him, in his Commons office: 'We've got to get rid of him.'

In 1969 Thorpe, Bessell and Holmes discuss it again, drawing up a plan to lure Scott to Cornwall to kill him. But how? Breaking his neck was considered impractical. Shooting him made sense, but how to dispose of a body on open moorland? Poisoning risked him dropping dead in a country pub. Other ideas apparently floated included throwing Scott down a tin mine. Or into fast-setting concrete. Or into an alligator-filled swamp in Florida. All are dropped. They would have to think on it.

In the February 1974 general election the Liberals win 6 million votes, almost trebling the total from four years earlier and one in five of the total number cast. It is an extraordinary reversal of fortunes for a party which had fallen a long way from its nineteenth-century heyday. The result means Conservative PM Edward Heath is out, but Harold Wilson's Labour Party is deprived of an overall majority. Thorpe comes very close to entering government with Heath – he leaves his house by the back door and runs across a muddy field to avoid photographers as he dashes to London for talks. They came to nothing. A second election is likely that year, and with it a real prospect of Liberals entering government. If Scott goes public – or more accurately, succeeds in getting people to listen to his increasingly public pronouncements – Thorpe's ministerial career would be over before it starts.

Enter John Le Mesurier – not the one who played Sergeant Wilson in *Dad's Army* (even this story isn't that mad) but a carpet salesman from Bridgend. A friend of Holmes, he introduces the plotters to George Deakin, a fruit machine salesman from South Wales, who in turn uses a boozy night at a Blackpool hotel to recruit Andrew 'Gino' Newton, a 29-year-old airline pilot. It is claimed that they discussed killing Scott for a fee of between £5,000 and £10,000. Crucially, Thorpe helps raise the money.

A trained hitman Newton is not. Told to head for Barnstaple in Devon, he initially sets off for Dunstable, some 200 miles east. Having finally found Scott, he lures him onto Exmoor by telling him someone is trying to kill him, which is at least accurate. By this stage Mrs Tish is long dead (put down after attacking some chickens), but Scott has a new dog, a Great Dane named Rinka, which he takes along for protection. It is a wet night on 24 October 1975 when they drive from Combe Martin, outside Barnstaple, to Porlock so that Newton (posing as a man called Peter Keene) can carry out some unspecified business. On the return journey, the car slowly climbs Porlock Hill, the steepest A-road in Britain (which anybody who has driven an overloaded ice-cream van up that stretch will attest. Oh, just me?)

Newton begins driving erratically, ineptly trying to find the spot he had earlier marked for the execution. Scott, who does not have a driving licence, bizarrely offers to take over and Newton, even more bizarrely, agrees. As Scott gets out of the car to swap seats, Rinka also leaps out, presumably thinking it is time for walkies. So Newton does what any highly trained assassin would do and shoots the dog. He turns to Scott and tells him it is his turn. But, in keeping with the sense of professionalism which is the hallmark of this operation, the gun jams. 'I can hear that noise in my hair, him trying to make it work,' Scott told *The Sunday Times* almost half a century later. 'The dog shouldn't have been there. Had the dog not been there, that bullet would have killed me.' Newton drives off, leaving Scott in the pouring rain clutching his dead dog and trying to wave down a passing car.

In the years that followed Newton went to prison for his role in the dog shooting, and Scott was charged with a social security fraud, using both court cases to make claims about Thorpe from the dock. Just to add to the outlandishness of this sorry tale, at one point Harold Wilson suggested to the Commons that he thought the stories about Thorpe's private life might be the work of the South African secret service: 'I have no doubt at all that there is strong South African participation in recent activities relating to the right honourable gentleman, the Leader of the Liberal Party.' As pressure mounted, two months later, in May 1976, Thorpe resigned as Liberal leader.

On 4 August 1977 Thorpe was charged, along with Holmes and two others, with conspiracy to murder Scott. In the trial that eventually followed in spring 1979, almost two decades after Thorpe met Scott, Mr Justice Cantley's extraordinarily biased summing-up described Scott as 'a hysterical, warped personality, a fraud, sponger, whiner, parasite – but, of course, he could be telling the truth'. The jury acquitted all four defendants, but it is difficult to know the true impact of the judge's diatribe.

The verdict came on 22 June, exactly seven weeks after Thatcher had arrived in Downing Street as prime minister in an election in which Thorpe had lost his own seat while awaiting trial. Also standing in his North Devon seat was the writer and satirist Auberon Waugh, representing the Dog Lovers' Party. His leaflet 'Rinka is NOT forgotten. Rinka lives. Woof woof' was banned by the courts to prevent the pending trial being prejudiced by the press. That job, it seemed, belonged to the presiding judge.

Relieved, Thorpe left court 'wearing a brown trilby at a jaunty angle', *The Times* reported the next day. He was, perhaps, the last man in Britain still wearing a hat. Times had changed. The 1970s had been a decade in which the post-war consensus and deference had crumbled. Thorpe was a symbol of the grubbiness that had infected a political Establishment who had brought industrial action, social unrest and political chaos to a country by now crying out for change. Thatcher, as a woman and someone of impeccable personal background, promised to deliver it. In the 1979 election, the week before the trial, the Tories gained more than 3 million votes as they swept to power. The Liberals, now under David Steel, lost a million votes, and one seat to the Conservatives: North Devon. Fighting back tears, dejected Thorpe insisted in his concession speech: 'North Devon has been Liberal for 20 years, and it will be Liberal again.' Having composed himself, he took questions from reporters. Asked if his upcoming trial for conspiracy to murder might have played a part in his defeat, he remarked with characteristic optimism: 'I think it's much too early to say.'

*Travel*

# 45

# Newton-le-Willows, Liverpool and Manchester Railway

*Wednesday, 15 September 1830*

Politicians love a PR stunt. That much is not new. And when you're a thrusting prime minister keen to show that you are at the forefront of new thinking and technology, you want to get on board. The Duke of Wellington's trip to mark the opening of the pioneering Liverpool to Manchester Railway, the first steam-powered inter-city passenger service, should have been a triumph. Crowds turned out in their thousands to marvel at this travel break-through. Instead an accident on the line would leave a former cabinet minister dead, lead to uproar on the streets and risk putting Brit-ons off having anything to do with these newfangled railways.

At 11 a.m. on 15 September 1830, a procession of trains left Crown Street station in Liverpool. The prime minister, the Duke of Wellington, was to travel on a special train pulled by *Northum-brian*, the most advanced locomotive from that famous train wizz, George Stephenson. Seven other trains would travel on a parallel line, allowing them to over- and undertake during the journey inland to Manchester. Wellington's train was packed with dignitaries, celebrities and rail industry bosses.

Just before noon the *Northumbrian* stopped at Parkside, near Newton-le-Willows, to take on water and fuel. People got off to stretch their legs, despite being told not to. Two trains passed on the other line without any problems. Among those on the tracks by this time was William Huskisson, a Tory MP who had been in Wellington's cabinet before a falling-out years earlier but who had been asked along for the ride as a local MP for Liverpool, which would benefit from the new railways. Keen to make amends, Huskisson decided to go to the royal car and shake hands with Wellington.

Then a cry went up that a third train, Stephenson's *Rocket*, was hurtling down the track towards them. Men rushed to get back on board. In the melee, Huskisson dithered, panicked, clung to a carriage door which swung out, lost his balance, and fell. On the ground he tried to wriggle to safety, but made things worse. He somehow bent his left leg so it crossed the track twice, allowing the wheels of the *Rocket* to go over both his calf and his thigh. A blood-curdling scream cut through the late-morning air.

A carriage door was ripped off to be used as a makeshift stretcher. Handily there was a surgeon on board who started talking about amputation. 'This is my death,' Huskisson exclaimed. He wasn't wrong. He was transferred to another train to be taken to Manchester, where he made some changes to his will, and then, at 9.05 p.m., he died.

While Huskisson was whisked away, passengers in the prime minister's train were becoming embroiled in an increasingly bizarre row. Wellington and his home secretary, Robert Peel, wanted to cancel the rest of the trip. For an hour or more the issue was debated, before the railway directors pointed out that the people of Manchester would be disappointed, and talk of accidents and cancellations might not be very good PR for the new railways. So, amazingly, they put the business of someone dying behind them, and on they went. Arriving in Manchester around 3 p.m., Wellington's train was greeted by booing crowds hurling vegetables. The train left for the return trip to Liverpool after ninety minutes. The next day Wellington cancelled the rest of the planned festivities for his visit, including being given freedom of the city of Liverpool. Flags flew at half-mast. Shops closed. Liverpool remembered the great politician it had lost. It would be wrong to describe Huskisson as a man who made history. But he was one of the men who made some of the early steps that the history makers would follow in. And perhaps he might have done more, given the chance.

Huskisson served under five prime ministers of varying quality – Pitt, Goderich, Wellington, Canning and Liverpool – in a number of ministerial jobs, including Leader of the Commons, a role in which he succeeded one future prime minister in Canning, and was replaced by another, Peel. Perhaps his most significant role was as president of the Board of Trade, in which he sought to persuade Tory merchants of the merits of free trade over protectionist tariffs. Having introduced the Corn Laws, he later inched towards reforming them.

In the early nineteenth century, as politicians grappled with the slave trade, Huskisson was initially opposed to abolition – not least as an MP in a city like Liverpool, built on wealth generated by slavery. He later proposed the Consolidated Slave Law, a fudge of a bill passed in 1826 which did give slaves the right to both own property and give evidence in court, but also set out various circumstances in which a slave could be lawfully killed by a white person. Slavery would not be abolished in British law until 1833, three years after Huskisson's death.

For all his small marks on history, Huskisson, was accident-prone: if he could trip over it, he would. He had the unusual distinction of having both fallen off a horse, and separately been trapped under one. If he could break it, he had done and would do again. And he had been told not to attend the opening of the Liverpool to Manchester Railway, having recently undergone surgery and for six weeks lived on little more than tea and toast. But he was a big supporter of new technology, including the steam train. Britain must embrace the new, he believed, or be left behind.

And, ironically, his role that day helped. The publicity surrounding the accident meant that many more people heard about this new, cheap, fast form of transport and were undeterred by the small matter of an early fatality. Half a million people travelled on the Liverpool and Manchester line in its first year. Passengers have been complaining about services ever since, while politicians get the blame for the same delays and cancellations which beset the railway's first day.

As for Huskisson, *The Times* said after his death that he 'beyond all contemporary politicians, deserved the praise of being a practical statesman' and described him as a man 'so enlightened in his opinions, and so practised in affairs'. There were rumours at the time that Huskisson and his allies had been about to be returned to Wellington's cabinet. It could have marked the most important stage in his political career. Instead Huskisson secured his place in history as the first person to be killed by a steam train on the newly opened inter-city railways, cutting short a promising if unfulfilled career in this ultimate political sliding doors moment.

# 46

# Brighton to London train

*Summer 1972*

In politics, it's not always what you say, but how you say it. And in 1972 Margaret Thatcher knew that she had to do something about her voice. She was furious, if not a little hurt, at being dropped from a party-political broadcast when she was education secretary, apparently a result of complaints about her high pitch. In the macho, male-dominated world of 1970s politics, a woman's voice was both an unusual and an unloved thing. This negative judgement of a forceful woman, often disparaged as 'shrill', was well ingrained in the national psyche. Shakespeare wrote of Cordelia in *King Lear*: 'Her voice was ever soft, gentle, and low, an excellent thing in woman.'

A chance encounter meant that Thatcher got help from the most unlikely of places. Gordon Reece, a cigar-chomping TV producer-turned-Tory PR man, carried out polling after each interview and appearance to find out what people thought of her, and he knew the voice was a problem. The Lincolnshire schoolgirl had picked up bad habits at Oxford, poshing it up to fit in, as many do at university. As an adult it came across as old-fashioned, bossy and schoolmarmish. He would try, in vain, to soften her pronunciation and accent, running filmed sessions in which she would be forced to repeat stock phrases again and again and watch them back. Her despairing spin doctor peered through his oversized glasses and knew something must be done.

Reece was mulling this on a train journey from Brighton to London when he bumped into none other than Laurence Olivier, the legendary actor, who was by now running the National Theatre. The thesp would help Thatcher. They met once at Olivier's home in Hampstead, but characteristically he talked mostly about himself. More useful was the offer of the services of the National Theatre's voice coach Kate Fleming, who had helped Olivier to lower his voice by an octave in preparation for his acclaimed performances as Othello. (He once wrote her a note to thank her 'for the spitting exercises'.) Fleming also worked with Peter O'Toole, Anthony Hopkins, Diana Rigg, Mia Farrow, Derek Jacobi and Ian McKellen, who would all go on to global stardom.

Leafing through files in Fleming's archive, donated to the National Theatre in 2012, it becomes clear that, despite protestations to the contrary even from some of Thatcher's closest aides and friends, the Iron Lady did indeed have regular voice-coaching sessions. They lasted throughout the period from 1972, when she was education secretary and being derided as 'Thatcher the milk snatcher', through becoming Tory leader and leader of the opposition in February 1975, and on until late 1976.

One invoice from May 1973, sent to Peter Walker at Conservative Central Office in Smith Square, billed for '£37.80p for six lessons from October 1972 to February 1973'. There is also a letter from Reece on headed notepaper bearing the blue parliamentary portcullis above 'The Rt Hon. Mrs Margaret Thatcher, House of Commons, London SW1A 0AA'. It reveals that Reece had been 'chivvying' Fleming to put in a bill for her work, and adds: 'For the very extensive period over which you have assisted Mrs Thatcher, I think that we agreed that the sum would be £200. Could you also invoice "to group sessions, fee as agreed £200". Love, Gordon.' A separate compliments slip reveals that in December 1976 she was actually paid a cheque for £210 for these 'group sessions', which seems to have been a euphemism for what were actually personal voice lessons.

Rewatch old news clips and it is clear that it worked. Compare Thatcher's interviews from the early 1970s with those a decade later, and it could almost be two different people. Slower, more deliberate, and much, much lower. By some estimations, 46 hertz lower, putting her halfway between the average female and male voice. Clive James, the TV critic, wrote in the *Observer* in 1975 that the tone of her voice had long been a problem, 'the condescending explanatory whine which treats the squirming interlocutor as an eight-year-old child with personality deficiencies'. Charles Moore, Thatcher's biographer, told me that after the training she sounded 'somewhat artificial', but it gave her more gravitas 'without pretending to be a man'. He added: 'It gave her more staying power – you get very tired making public speeches and when it's coming more out of your stomach, and less at the top of your throat, that helps. She wasn't perhaps a natural orator in some ways, but the ability to whack the message home was pretty amazing.'

This was not just some act for the cameras either. It was a permanent change which remained even at home or in private. It had a transformative effect on the public impression of her. Along with changes to her hair and clothes, she became less feminine, arguably more male, which might have helped inch towards the public's idea of what a prime minister looked like – until she entered Downing Street in 1979 it had only ever been a man in a suit. Yet she retained sex appeal. Even today some Conservative men still go weak at the knees at the thought of her. A story goes that when a newspaper commented on her vocal makeover, Tory MP Jim Prior sidled up to her and said: 'Margaret, I read in my paper that you have developed a sexy voice.' To which she replied: 'And what makes you think I wasn't sexy before?'

In an interview during the 1979 election campaign, legendary BBC documentary maker Michael Cockerell questioned Thatcher about how her voice was 'much lower than it used to be'. She paused, 'Yes, um. Yes. I'm not quite sure why?' But she knew exactly why. And it was another woman who had helped her to find her voice.

# 47

# Helipad, Don Valley Bowl, Sheffield

*Wednesday, 1 April 1992*

O f course the helicopter was red. They had thought of every-thing. And as it came in to land just before dusk, 11,000 people were cheering a live video feed inside the Sheffield Arena on the other side of the field. They cheered again when Neil Kin-nock climbed out, and helped his wife Glenys down from the step. In fact they didn't stop cheering and clapping and whoop-ing and hollering for the whole night. They kept on cheering right up until the day Labour lost the election.

There are some who claim it was the Sheffield rally wot lost it. There are some, including Kinnock himself, who claim it was hailed as a great triumph at the time and only mocked after the 1992 election defeat to John Major. Both are, to varying degrees, wrong. But aside from the immediate impact in election terms, what Sheffield did do was put the brakes on an increasing Ameri-canisation of British politics: not the discourse but the disco, the music and lights and balloons and tickertape. Never again would a candidate to be prime minister hold a victory rally before vic-tory had actually been secured. Having attempted to put the party into political party, since then campaigning has been more stiff-upper-lip and less streamers and fireworks.

That April day, from mid-afternoon the buses started arriving, Labour supporters each having paid £1 to join what organisers called the 'Mega Rally', one week and one day before Britain went to the polls. That it was being held on April Fool's Day might have given Kinnock & co. pause to wonder if they risked looking daft, but new polls that day suggested that they could be on course to win a majority.

The shadow cabinet, described as the 'government-in-waiting', were introduced with the 'come on down' vibes of *The Price Is Right*, clapped in to the strains of Labour's election anthem 'My Land, Your Land'. Like boxers heading to the ring, they paraded along a red carpet which ran the length of the arena and onto the stage, beneath huge flags of the UK, England, Wales, Scotland, Northern Ireland and the EU, fluttering thanks to carefully positioned fans in the rafters. They had thought of everything.

There were celebrity video messages from the DJ Paul Gambaccini, the athlete Steve Cram, the astrophysicist Stephen Hawking and actors including Alan Rickman, Stephen Fry, Emma Thompson, John Mortimer and Sir Richard Attenborough. Simply Red's Mick Hucknall was filmed filling in his postal vote, singing his song 'Something Got Me Started' while praising the prospect of a Labour government which would 'invest in skills'. I swear this is all true. They had thought of everything, even the things which might have been better left unthought.

The music playlist seemed to have been designed by a committee tasked with appealing to all tastes, from opera to rock, modern jazz to traditional brass, and everything in between: bagpipers, the Frickley Colliery Band, Alison Limerick, and then there was Sarah Jane Morris from the Communards. Someone sang 'Summertime', then the jazz musician Courtney Pine and a gospel choir played 'Jerusalem' and everyone joined in.

If you were being polite, you would say people were just a bit giddy at the thought of a Labour government after thirteen years of Thatcher and Major. In truth, some of them lost the plot.

Three times Kinnock's deputy Roy Hattersley said: 'Labour has won the election.' John Smith, the shadow chancellor, did some topical comedy: 'Starring John Major, the Conservative's very own box office disaster: *Honey, I Shrunk the Economy.*' The biggest ovation, though, went to Barbara Castle, introduced as 'the First Lady of Socialism'.

Then the big screen showed Kinnock's bright-red helicopter hovering into view, and somehow the atmosphere was cranked up further. Fireworks. Streamers. Glitter. Kinnock himself was dressed soberly in a dark suit, dark spotted tie and a red rose on his lapel. But there was nothing sober about his performance. One thing they hadn't thought of was how Kinnock would start his speech.

'We're all right!' he bellowed. 'We're all right! We're all right!' But did he? Kinnock himself insists it was a 'completely inane rock and roll concert cry of "Well all right."' Hmmm. Several papers at the time, including *The Daily Telegraph*, reported him saying 'We're all right.' The playwright David Hare in his account of the campaign, *Asking Around*, had it as just 'A'right.' David Butler and Dennis Kavanagh, in *The British General Election of 1992*, said Kinnock 'shouted to the crowd like a pop-star "You're all ri', you're all ri."' *The Sunday Telegraph* reported it as 'Yerallriiiiiight?,' in a piece in which James Langton said the rally was 'all spotlights and schadenfreude'. Kinnock used his content-free speech to declare with certainty: 'In nine days' time Britain is going to have a Labour government.' It wasn't.

Once offstage things went less according to plan. The group of journalists following Kinnock during the campaign boarded a bus to East Midlands airport, but it got stuck in mud. The replacement broke down. A third one was sent for. It meant Labour's campaign plane, carrying the leader and his aides, had to wait and wait, the *Liverpool Echo* reported. *Red Rose One*, the hilariously naff nickname for Kinnock's private plane, finally took off at 12.20 a.m., almost two hours late. Kinnock struggling to take off after a glitzy rally was one for metaphors fans.

Labour insiders, keen to burnish their European credentials, had briefed that the event was inspired by rallies held by the French socialist President François Mitterrand. Observers took a different view. Michael Brunson, on the ITV *News at Ten*, said it 'was the nearest British equivalent to an American-style convention'. The BBC's John Cole, reporting from inside the event, said: 'This rally is undoubtedly the most astounding political meeting I've seen since Kennedy's attempt to win the Democratic nomination in New York in 1960.' Tim Ewart reported for ITN: 'This was not the Republican Party of America, but the Labour Party of Great Britain.'

Three decades on, Kinnock tries to play down the Americanisation of Labour's operation, insisting to me that Sheffield was 'entirely authentic, not the invented excitement of American stuff. We, thank God, are still a long way from that complete razzle-dazzle nonsense.' The use of the helicopter in Labour colours was 'incidental', he says: 'I had to – it was the only way I could get there in time.' He does, though, concede that Sheffield may have got out of hand: 'The people who organised it decided that we were going to be presented as the next cabinet. And since then I've often introduced myself as "My name is Neil Kinnock, I used to be the next prime minister" because it was so ridiculously overdone. But that didn't matter as it happened, because it was reported in a fairly sober and favourable way. So it's only weeks afterwards that the mythology was invented.'

This, though, is myth-making too. It was widely reported at the time, a week before the election, and not everyone thought it a good idea. Far from being underplayed, it was the splash, front-page photo and page-one sketch in *The Guardian*. Andrew Rawnsley's sketch began: 'Labour gave a party last night to celebrate winning the general election. The fact that seven campaigning days stand between Neil Kinnock and Number 10 was treated as an incidental detail.'

The front page of *The Telegraph* called it a 'presidential-style rally', while on page four Jon Hibbs wrote: 'There was no dry ice, but there were no dry eyes by the end either.' Caroline Davies in the London *Evening Standard* called it an 'all-American extravaganza', adding: 'From the glitz and hype at this £150,000 mega-rally to the £2 hotdogs, the Sheffield Arena show had all the hallmarks of a US import . . . Premature perhaps, but this was definitely a victory party.' A cartoon by Jak in the same paper showed Kinnock on a big screen addressing uniformed guards holding Labour banners featuring hammers and sickles. It prompted complaints.

Kenneth Baker, the Conservative home secretary, was among those sent on the attack: 'Huge amounts of what looked like glitter fluttered from the ceiling. Actually it was shredded banknotes symbolically representing what Labour would do to the British economy.' Michael Heseltine, the environment secretary, and not a man known for his frugality, mocked the largesse: 'The gleaming cars! The luxury coaches! The walkie-talkies for Neil Kinnock's minders! I have never seen such luxury! The new Jerusalem paid for by £500-a-head nosh-ups for the London glitterati!' The next day's papers reported that £5 billion had been wiped off the value of shares as the City panicked at the apparent inevitability of a Labour victory. The Lib Dems picking up in the polls, and the prospect of their leader Paddy Ashdown acting as kingmaker, also spooked the markets, and the public.

Major, by contrast, was going back to basics, addressing voters from a soapbox in the drizzle. No televised Tory-branded helicopter here. The day after the Sheffield rally, Kinnock was asked at a press conference about Labour's showy campaign compared to Major in his anorak. 'Come on, be fair,' Kinnock shot back. 'It's not an anorak, it's a second-rate Barbour.' Which is probably not quite the putdown he thought it was.

Matthew Parris, the *Times* sketchwriter, was so incensed by the briefing given to journalists on the exact timings of the rally ('17.30 doors open, party bus, band etc. arrive. Street entertainers will be working the audience outside') that he left the city before it had even finished. But, presciently, he wondered in the sketch

he filed from the train if the 'slick, sick, cynical image manipula-
tion of Labour's spectacular' might elicit not voter excitement
but contempt: 'Last night in Sheffield, image throttled intellect
and a quiet voice in every reporter present whispered that there
was something disgusting about the occasion. These voices will
grow.' And grow they did. Later Dennis Skinner, the left-winger
firebrand, would claim that the event had 'destroyed in ten seconds eight years' practice by Mr Kinnock at being a statesman'.
He was proved right.

On Thursday, 9 April 1992, eight days after the Sheffield rally,
Britain went to the polls. The Conservatives lost 40 seats, but
shocked many by retaining a majority, the fourth in a row. Major
had secured 14,093,007 votes, more than any party leader before
or since. The *Newcastle Journal* found one other big winner: David
Hutchinson, a 51-year-old antiques exporter from Throckley,
Newcastle, had put a £500 bet on a Conservative majority at 7–1
just two days before polling day. He won £4,000. 'It was that
Sheffield rally that did it for me,' he told the paper. 'When I saw
all that triumphalism on the telly I knew Kinnock wasn't going
to win.'

In the defeat's post-mortems that word, 'triumphalism',
cropped up again and again. Reporter James Langton later admitted that at the time the rally 'looked like a masterstroke, a piece
of breath-taking audacity', but now it would be seen as 'a huge
mistake, a symbol of the image-makers gone berserk on a massive scale. It was not the British way of politics.' No, it was just
too American. These days we get pale, embarrassed party staff
wearing XL logo-ed T-shirts over their shirts and ties. Sometimes party HQ has printed their vacuous slogan on a sign or
two for staff to hold up reluctantly for the benefit of the cameras.
But never again anything on the scale of Sheffield, and with that,
we're all right.

# 48

# Hinton Airfield, Northamptonshire

*Thursday May 6, 2010*

'Oh fuck.' As famous last words they were unlikely to make it into the history books for their elegance or originality, but as a soundbite to sum up the mood in the face of imminent death, it did the job. After muttering the expletive under his breath, Nigel Farage did something unusual for him: he stopped talking. He contemplated phoning loved ones, but what do you say? A send-to-all text message was too impersonal. A final cigarette? Too dangerous when surrounded by jet fuel. So he sat quietly and watched the ground hurtle towards him.

It was an election stunt so old-fashioned as to be in keeping with the retro vibes of the pin-striped Eurosceptic who wanted to take Britain out of the EU and back to the good old days: a banner flown behind a small plane. It is the sort of thing you see at the seaside, or over a lower league football match. High-tech, it was not, and nor, it turned out, was it safe.

By May 2010 Farage had been a Member of the European Parliament for eleven years, and had spent three of them as leader of the UK Independence Party. He had tried, unsuccessfully, to become an MP five times already (in Eastleigh

in 1994, Salisbury in 1997, Bexhill and Battle in 2001, South
Thanet in 2005 and Bromley and Chislehurst in 2006). Hoping
it might be sixth time lucky, he stepped back from being party
leader to commit to a proper run for the Commons in 2010.

He chose, of the 650 seats available, to stand in Buckingham,
notable because the sitting MP there was John Bercow, the
former Tory MP who had been Commons Speaker since June
2009. By convention the main parties did not stand against the
independent Speaker, so Bercow would have expected a clear
run at re-election.

Farage spotted an opportunity, both for publicity and the
prospect of victory, claiming that MPs had 'broken the trust' of
the British people and that Bercow 'represents all that is wrong
with British politics today. He was embroiled in the expenses
saga, and he presides over a Parliament that virtually does
nothing.' Some pundits said Farage had a decent chance of victory but it would be a challenge. Without being party leader, he
would struggle to attract media attention during a nationwide
general election.

Which is why he decided to take to the skies. Early on polling
day, Thursday, May 6, Farage headed to the airfield at Hinton-
in-the-Hedges, just outside the Buckingham constituency.
Around the same time Justin Adams landed a navy-blue Wilga
35A two-seater plane, having flown in from Winchester.
Adams was to criss-cross the skies over the polling stations of
Buckingham, with a banner fluttering behind the plane declaring: 'Vote for your country – Vote Ukip.' Farage had decided to
go with him – not that anybody looking skyward from the
ground would have been able to see that the candidate was in
the cockpit. Neil Hall, a local agency photographer, had arrived
to take pictures, although as it was polling day and broadcasters
are limited in what they can show, there was otherwise very
little media interest.

Banner-flying, though, is a complicated business. Instead
of hurtling down a runway with the slogan already attached

like tin cans on a wedding car, the plane takes off, does a loop and then swoops down to hook up the banner which is stretched between two poles ten feet off the ground. Adams circled then dipped the plane down, and missed. He went round again, and missed. And again. And again. It was only on the fifth attempt that the plane's hook finally picked up the banner. Success.

'This is an emergency,' Adams shouted, looking over his shoulder. 'Real trouble.' The banner had got itself wrapped around the plane's rudder and tail. A crash landing seemed unavoidable. It was at this moment that Farage uttered his two-word valedictory, and then fell silent. Adams was sweating profusely as he grappled with the rodeo ride of the plane's controls, while also making emergency calls on the radio. The two men, shoulders touching in the tiny plane, just cleared a hedge, then the banner hit the ground and the plane lurched forwards to follow it. Farage shut his eyes, not expecting to ever open them again.

Upside down in the cockpit and paralysed with pain, blood dripping across his face, Farage could smell fuel and the fear kicked in. As help arrived, Farage shouted: 'I'm scared! I'm scared! Get me out of this fucking thing.' As he staggered from the wreckage, Hall began taking photos. Farage reached into his pocket and took out a packet of Rothmans, asking aide Duncan Barkes to light it for him, but with broken ribs and a chipped spine he could only manage a few drags before stamping it out on the floor. He was taken to hospital, drifting in and out of consciousness.

The fire brigade had to cut the wreckage to free Adams, who was badly affected by the ordeal and subsequent aviation inquiry. Although he was cleared of any wrong-doing, he suffered from alcoholism and mental ill-health, and was later convicted of making threats to kill Farage. He died in 2013, still haunted by what happened on the airfield that day.

The pictures of Farage clambering from the carnage, in his navy suit, pale-blue shirt and striped tie, went around the world. His contorted, confused and blood-stained face was almost unrecognisable. One of the most prominent politicians in the country had had a lucky escape. He was less lucky in the election. Bercow won comfortably with 22,860 votes, with Farage on 8,410 pushed into third behind a local campaigner called John Stevens who secured 10,331 votes.

Having recovered from the crash over the summer, Farage returned as Ukip leader in November that year and would spend the next two and a half years piling pressure on the Conservatives to promise a referendum on Britain's place in the EU – a promise David Cameron made in January 2013, and famously delivered in 2016.

I have always retained doubts that it was Farage who won the Brexit referendum – indeed the main Vote Leave campaign distanced themselves from Farage's anti-immigrant populism and his weird bunch of cronies like Arron Banks, who busied themselves during the campaign with chaotic social media posts and organising rallies with ageing popstars who promptly pulled out when they found out what it was for.

Yet it is hard to argue that the EU referendum would have happened at all without Farage being around to push for it. The beer-swilling, straight-talking, grinning frog in a velvet-collared coat had an electoral appeal that none of his Ukip colleagues, or indeed many of his opponents, could match. Ukip's ability to deny Tory MPs of their majorities was a key factor in the party's slide into Euroscepticism. They did not need to become MPs themselves in order to change the politics of the Commons.

Which is lucky, as Farage never managed it. He ran again once more in 2015, back in South Thanet, and came 2,812 votes behind the Tory candidate Craig Mackinlay. It was a contest best remembered for comedian Al Murray standing in the seat as his Pub Landlord character. Farage did not seem to know what to make of this blazer-wearing, pint-pulling self-publicist. But he never went up in a plane with a banner again.

# 49

# M11 speed camera, Essex

*Wednesday, 12 March 2003*

The Liberal Democrats were in crisis mode. One of their cabinet ministers was to go on trial charged with conspiracy to pervert the course of justice. So naturally the first person to address the party's great and good was a six-foot man dressed as a bee.

It was either fortuitous or terrible timing that when news came through of the prosecution of Chris Huhne, then energy and climate change secretary, all the party's ministers, MPs and senior advisers were together at a weekend retreat in Eastbourne. Huhne himself, not a man known to have ever hidden his light under a bushel, had turned up on the first day but was sent away by spin doctors fearing a PR disaster. Late morning the next day, Friday, 3 February 2012, MPs were gathered in the meeting room of the smart Hydro Hotel listening to a dull presentation about the environment. Actually no, not listening. Deputy prime minister Nick Clegg, like everybody else in the room, was glued to his phone checking for updates on Huhne's case. Steve Webb, the pensions minister, was the one who broke it to colleagues, with a gloomy thumbs-down gesture. Bizarrely, the presentation still continued for another quarter of an hour.

Clegg spoke sombrely to his MPs, and then left with aides. The mood among Lib Dems was grim. Then the door flew open and in walked Barnaby the Bee. A black and yellow foam body and head, smiley face, googly eyes and protruding antennae all atop a pair of black-stockinged legs. 'Can I introduce you all to the Eastbourne Buzz!' bellowed Stephen Lloyd, the local MP, who wasn't going to let the small matter of his party's political and legal meltdown get in the way of having senior colleagues pose for photos with his massive mascot. Recalling the surreal scene now, Lloyd tells me: 'Barnaby Bee, who puts the buzz back into Bournemouth, got a bigger bloody round of applause than the deputy prime minister.' MPs and ministers quietly left, some joking that they could do with the insect costume to avoid the waiting cameras outside, and set off on the drive home, taking care to abide by the speed limit, obviously. It was nine years earlier that Huhne had not been so careful.

Each week of his six years as MEP for the South East of England Huhne would fly home from Brussels and then drive south from Stansted airport to London along the M11. Shortly before 11.30 p.m. on Wednesday, 12 March 2003 his black BMW was flashed by a speed camera at Chigwell in Essex, doing more than 20 mph above the legal limit. This was a problem because the habitual speeder was already close to the maximum and three more points would likely lead to a ban and prosecution. And this in turn was a problem because he was in the process of campaigning to become an MP in Eastleigh, Hampshire. So the then-48-year-old asked his economist wife, Vicky Pryce, 50, to take the points for him, telling the police she had been driving that night. She signed the form and the problem went away.

Except in June 2010, just weeks after the coalition had been formed and Huhne had become one of five Lib Dem cabinet ministers, it emerged he had been having an affair with his former press officer, Carina Trimingham. He broke the news to his family during half-time of a World Cup match, before writing a press statement and going to the gym. Humiliated, Pryce filed for divorce on the grounds of adultery, in what became a particularly acrimonious split after 26 years of marriage. She was out for vengeance, at any cost, but perhaps even she did not expect to land herself in jail too. Initially she told *The Mail on Sunday* that Huhne had passed the points to a constituency aide, Jo White, but it quickly became clear that White had not started driving until the year after the M11 speeding offence. Whoops. Pryce moved on to *The Sunday Times*, and over lunch with its political editor, Isabel Oakeshott, she spilled the beans about the points-swap. On Sunday, 8 May 2011 *The Sunday Times* and *The Mail on Sunday* ended up splashing the same claim from Pryce that Huhne had pressured 'somebody' into taking the points. It did not take long before it emerged that the 'somebody' was Pryce herself.

The case moved at a rather more sedate pace than the Huhne-mobile, and it was nine months later that news came through to the Eastbourne awayday that Huhne and his ex would both be charged with perverting the course of justice. The director of public prosecutions at the time was one Keir Starmer, who appeared on TV warning: 'Can I remind all concerned that Mr Huhne and Ms Pryce now stand charged with criminal offences and that they each have a right to a fair trial. It is very important that nothing is said, or reported, which could prejudice their trial.' Huhne quit the cabinet immediately but remained an MP until the trial began, when he suddenly pleaded guilty on the first day – a year and a day after first being charged. Pryce pleaded not guilty on the grounds of marital coercion, but the jury found her guilty too.

Both lives were in ruins, careers in tatters, a family shattered. Of all the examples of the butterfly effect of tiny personal mis-judgements having huge political ramifications, this must rank near the top. Huhne was a highly rated politician, and no one rated him more highly than himself. A former journalist who enjoyed reminding interviewers of this fact, he also loved to roll out anecdotes about his expertise as an economist, City highflyer, bond market expert, MEP and linguist. He was pathologically incapable of having a conversation about politics without making sly, and not so sly, digs at his rivals and even colleagues.

In 2006, three years after getting flashed by that speed camera, he had run for the Lib Dem leadership following Charles Kennedy's resignation. He was beaten by Clegg by just 511 votes, with delayed postal votes perhaps meaning he would have actually won. So it could have been the deputy prime minister doing jail time. In another parallel universe where he remained in the cabinet beyond 2012 he could have been a challenger to Clegg in government. At the 2015 election he might have had a better plan to prevent the Lib Dem wipeout. He would definitely have thought he did. Instead, in May 2013, after serving sixty-two days of his eight-month sentence, he left Leyhill Prison. His political career was over two years earlier even than those of his Lib Dem colleagues who would go on to be thrown out by the voters. Unlike six-foot Barnaby the Bee, that must have really stung.

# 50

# A4, Great West Road, Chiswick

*Friday, 14 October 2022*

Fuller's Brewery has operated on the corner of the M4 and A4 in Chiswick since 1845, back in the days when Robert Peel's Conservative government was bitterly divided over the merits of free trade. Kwasi Kwarteng's motorcade had just passed the landmark beer house when he learnt that his own brief experiment in free-market economics to solve the cost-of-living crisis was about to come to an end. He found out he was being sacked as chancellor of the exchequer while reading a tweet in the back of his government car, a grey Range Rover Discovery. After just thirty-eight days in the Treasury, his old friend Liz Truss was calling time on his job in a desperate attempt to save her own. Like so many Truss initiatives, it didn't work.

Truss and Kwarteng go way back. Both elected in 2010, from the back benches they championed low-tax, free-market economics before beginning their ascent to the top. 'We were mates,' Kwarteng tells me. Truss had been a minister for a decade, including as environment secretary, justice secretary, trade secretary and foreign secretary when, in summer 2022, she ran to replace Boris Johnson as prime minister. Her campaign was unapologetically pro-growth, arguing in favour of cutting both tax and red tape in order, in her view, to set the economy free.

Kwarteng was business secretary in Johnson's cabinet, and he spent much of August working on Truss's economic plans at Chevening, the grace-and-favour home she had use of as foreign secretary. He was '90 per cent certain' that he would be her chancellor. He was confirmed in the role when Truss beat Rishi Sunak to become PM on 6 September. Two days later Queen Elizabeth II died, and the country – and politics – entered a period of national mourning. Behind the scenes Truss used this time to beef up her economic plans. 'I think the funeral and the drama around a new monarch put people's heads in completely the wrong place,' says Kwarteng. There was a big debate about freezing or cutting spending. 'It was her view that it would just create a whole political nightmare. My fault is I was too indulgent of that. I should have made more arguments against what she was trying to do, particularly on spending. The markets would have worn that.'

By the time Kwarteng stood up in the Commons on 23 September, his so-called mini-Budget was not so mini. As he puts it, it was 'like a Christmas tree' with too many unfunded, pro-growth baubles hanging from it. So in addition to keeping leadership campaign promises to reverse Sunak's policy of hiking corporation tax to 25 per cent and the creation of a National Insurance levy to raise money for the NHS, he went further. Much further. A £45 billion package of tax cuts – the biggest for half a century – included a stamp duty cut, a 1p cut in the basic rate of income tax and the scrapping of the top rate of income tax, all unfunded and paid for from increased borrowing. The Office for Budget Responsibility had not been allowed to crunch the numbers. There was lots of talk of 'supply-side reform' but no detail, and it was soon being cast by critics as a rush-to-the-bottom bonfire of work, safety and environmental protections.

It was also just days after Truss and Kwarteng had unveiled a multi-billion-pound energy bill package to cap household costs, and it came just as central banks around the world were moving to hike interest rates to curb the inflation being fuelled by gas price rises following the Russian invasion of Ukraine. The market reaction to the mini-Budget was swift, and brutal. The pound crashed to its lowest level since 1985, banks cranked up interest rates on new mortgages, and the Bank of England stepped in to buy government bonds as the pensions market teetered. Kwarteng says he told her to 'slow down' at a time when currencies around the world were crashing. She did not listen. 'There was just too much.'

On Tuesday, 11 October Kwarteng took Treasury questions in the Commons, before heading to the annual meeting of finance ministers at the International Monetary Fund in Washington DC. There had been some debate about whether he should attend with the crisis burning at home, but it was decided that dodging the IMF would spook the markets further. The late booking and awkward flight times meant catching a plane to New York, staying overnight, and then boarding a train to the US capital early the next morning to be there on time. He was forced to sit through endless meetings in which officials told him his plans were crazy. In interviews Kwasi insisted: 'I am not going anywhere.' In fact, he was getting texts and calls from home. Truss and her team were demanding he cut short his trip, despite the very act of returning early being almost certain to add to the sense of chaos. In his absence, she had used Prime Minister's Questions to insist she was 'absolutely' ruling out any spending cuts. 'What Liz was brilliant at was adding fuel to the flames,' Kwarteng says bluntly. 'There was no drama that she wouldn't turn into a crisis. I just think Number 10 went into a blind panic.' He boarded the seven-hour overnight flight home thinking that there was a chance he would be fired, but 'the rational part of my brain thought this is mad'. Rumours had, however, reached Washington that Sajid Javid, who spent seven months as Boris Johnson's chancellor, was being lined up for the job.

British Airways flight BA292 was being tracked by more than 6,000 people as it performed a U-turn over the Surrey Hills (one for metaphor collectors) before landing at Heathrow at 10.50 a.m.

Kwarteng was quickly in his government car and being whisked into central London. They had just turned onto the A4 in Chiswick when sitting next to the chancellor Celia McSwaine, Kwarteng's special adviser, scrolled through Twitter. 'Oh,' she said. 'You've been sacked.' At 11.28 a.m. Steven Swinford, the impeccably sourced political editor of *The Times*, had tweeted: 'I'm told that Kwasi Kwarteng is being sacked as Chancellor as Liz Truss prepares to reverse the mini-Budget. Not clear who will be replacing him. Events moving very, very quickly this morning. No 10 not commenting.' Shortly after midday Kwarteng arrived in Downing Street, entering through a back door away from the glare of the cameras, and was taken straight into the cabinet room where he sat across the table from Truss. They were alone.

'It was just the two of us. I was slightly taken aback, but I could see where this was going.' Truss explained that, despite their long friendship, he had to go to save her, adding: 'They're already coming for me Kwasi.' Kwarteng recalls: 'She was crying. And I said, "This is nuts because they're going to ask you, if you've sacked him, why are you still there?" And she didn't say anything. She was literally in tears. I was very much of the view that she didn't have the temperament for the job. You don't cry when you sack people.' A spokesman for Truss denied that she cried during the meeting, and disputes Kwarteng's recollection of what was said.

By the time they met Kwarteng had in fact been out of a job for hours: it was at 9.30 a.m., with Kwarteng still somewhere over the Atlantic, that Truss had offered his job to Jeremy Hunt, who was on holiday in Belgium and returned to London to take up his post at 4 p.m. Kwarteng left office after just thirty-eight days as chancellor, only just beating Tory Iain Macleod who managed thirty days before he died in 1970.

That afternoon Truss made perhaps her oddest public appearance, a title for which there is stiff competition. In an eight-minute press conference she declared that 'the mission remains the same' before announcing that actually the mission was being torn up, and corporation tax would increase to 25 per cent after all, as Sunak had planned, raising £18 billion per year. She seemed weirdly spaced out. 'I met the former chancellor earlier today,' she said, getting her tenses muddled. 'I was incredibly sorry to lose him. He is a great friend.' She took only four questions, all of them, exactly as Kwarteng had predicted, asking why she thought she should stay in the job. Between each answer and calling the next she gave out a pained 'er . . .' like she was stuck on a maths puzzle and gazed, head tilted, at the room of smirking hacks.

'Can you explain why you think you should remain as prime minister,' gently inquired Ben Riley-Smith from the Truss-backing *Telegraph*. She burbled a jargon-filled non-response. 'How come you get to stay?' asked *The Sun*'s Harry Cole. Burble. The BBC's Chris Mason ventured: 'Excuse the bluntness, but given everything that has happened what credibility do you have to continue governing?' Gulp. Burble burble. Then she looked up one last time: 'Er . . . Robert Peston?' The ITV man asked if she would apologise to her party. She ignored it like all the other questions, burbled again about delivery and difficult decisions and economic stability, and then tottered off to consider her own political instability. 'That performance was so wooden,' one senior Conservative texted me. 'Getting rid of her wouldn't be regicide, it would be deforestation.' They wouldn't have to wait long to see her felled.

The next day Hunt went on Saturday morning TV to tear up the rest of the mini-Budget, vowing to reverse it all. The following Tuesday the home secretary, Suella Braverman, resigned for leaking government policy to allies. At PMQs the next day Truss declared: 'I am a fighter not a quitter,' but within hours was embroiled in a whipping row about a baffling Commons vote on fracking, which culminated in confusion over whether or not her chief whip Wendy Morton had resigned. There was also the fall-out of the Bank of England having to buy up £65 billion in government bonds to tackle a crisis sweeping through the pensions industry, which Truss claims she was never warned about.

Her advisers insist that this was the real cause of the economic meltdown, and hilariously claim the fact it happened after her mini-budget was 'just a coincidence'.

Enough was enough. The next day, just after lunch on Thursday, 20 October, Truss emerged from Downing Street to the spot where just forty-five days earlier she had set out her dreams as a new prime minister and announced she was quitting to end the nightmare. It turns out you can't brutally sack your chancellor, tear up your entire economic agenda and still survive. What is surprising is that Truss was no novice: she had been a minister for a decade, in some of the biggest jobs. One senior Number 10 official who worked with both Johnson and Truss says that the clues were there: 'With both Boris and Liz, in their ascent there were always people saying no – and when they got to the top they were untrammelled, there were no guard rails.'

Kwarteng agrees: 'I think her view is that she was always on the periphery. So she thought, "Now I have finally got control of the whole machine and I am just going to do what I want." She just went hell for leather. She should have reversed all the things, and then maybe sacked me a month afterwards or shuffled me out. But there's never any method with her. It's all shock and awe, rip everything up. It's that lack of temperament where you're rushing everything, and then once you get into a bit of a hole you lack the temperament to see your way out of it. Both getting into the mess, and then blowing up once you've got into the mess, were signs of the instability. A cooler person would have got out of the problems, but they probably wouldn't have got into them in the first place.' The price paid by the country was huge. The price paid by the low-tax free marketeers, who saw their long-held dreams shattered, remains high too. While Truss's departure set a new record for prime ministerial precarity, little of what unfolded was truly unique or unprecedented. The parallels echo down through a quarter of a millennium of political history. Like so many of the stories in these pages, it was a combination of hubris, haplessness and happenstance which changed British politics once more. Some are born to change, some achieve change, and some have change thrust upon them. And some are like Truss and Kwarteng. When they finally got the chance to change politics, they showed that they couldn't even organise a piss-up in a brewery on the A4.

# Acknowledgements

This book would not exist without my brilliant Times Radio listeners. The day that English Heritage reported a 20 per cent rise in visitors to Barnard Castle, we started talking on my show about other obscure sites of special political interest. Alternative destinations flooded in. This sowed the seed of an idea, which I blurted out a few days later to HarperCollins' Arabella Pike, who concluded this was finally one of my ideas for a book which would work. That all that talk came to something is the result of her patience and perseverance as an editor. Alex Gingell kept the pages turning as the project manager, proofreaders Linden Lawson and Richard Collins saved me from my mistakes, Julian Humphries made the outside of the book look as good as Jacqui Caulton made the inside, Chris Wright and Chris Gurney kept production on track, Sam Harding made things happen behind the scenes, and marketing supremo Matt Clacher and publicists Katherine Patrick and Lizzie Rowles made sure people knew about it when it was finally finished.

Across my various day jobs, I must thank my numerous bosses, including at Times Radio Tim Levell, and Stig Abell, and at *The Times* John Witherow, Tony Gallagher, Jeremy Griffin, and most significantly Emma Tucker, who from the day I joined *The Times* in 2016 encouraged me to say yes to everything – from podcasts and sketches to panels and stand-up – and for all I have done since she deserves the credit/blame. Writing this book has been an unexpected joy, but I am conscious that it has sometimes taken me away from the day job, so apologies to Roland Watson, Nicola Jeal and anyone else to whom I have filed late or not at all.

My incredible Times Radio team have, over many months, pretended not to be sick of hearing about this book and instead offered support, inspiration and encouragement, especially Andrew Alexander, Lewis Decker, Dominic Hauschild, Kea Browning, Erin Carney, Andrew Wright and Einar Orn. Thanks also to all of my *Times* and *Sunday Times* colleagues, not least Steven Swinford, Oliver Wright, Chris Smyth, George Grylls, Geri Scott, Tim Shipman and Gabriel Pogrund, for providing ideas, titbits and phone numbers.

I am indebted to Henry Zeffman and Patrick Maguire, two of the most talented political journalists I know, for reading not just my many drafts but also every WhatsApp message posted at all times of the day and night. I will never have the same weird level of political knowledge as them, but researching this book has helped me understand more of their obscure references. Lara Spirit has been characteristically enthusiastic, while offering nuggets of exactly the sort of colour and detail which make a book like this work. Daniel Finkelstein is as generous with his time as he is honest with his feedback; it is a privilege to count him as a friend. Ever since our Big Day Out sketch group days, Lewis Georgeson and William Kenning, my comedy brothers, have made me laugh through many hairbrained, over-ambitious projects of which this is just the latest. To my actual brother, Lee, thank you for providing the quiet support that neither of us would admit to out loud. Much of what I've done would have been less fun without Andrew Dunne, Chris Jordan, Alex Thompson, Charlie Howarth, Richard Edwards, Ria Broadbent, Graeme Demianyk, Oliver Barrett, Harry Griffin and Callie Chapman.

Thank you to everyone who spoke to me on or off the record for the book, or during the past two decades covering politics. In particular I would like to thank Kieran Andrews, Ed Balls, Chris Brannigan, Rory Carroll, Sam Coates, Michael Crick, Francis Elliott, Nigel Fletcher, William Hague, Ian Hislop, Iona Kielhorn, Kwasi Kwarteng, Shaun Ley, Alan Leaman, Adam Macqueen, Tom McTague, Lindsay McIntosh, Jane Merrick,

Charles Moore, David Owen, Mark Pack, John Stevens, Rachel Sylvester, David Torrance and Nick Thomas-Symonds. A special thanks to Mark Roodhouse for sharing so much of his work on Henry Durant, who does not get the credit he deserves for bringing polling to Britain. Thanks also to MJ Jennings and Nick Mays from The Times Archive, also the National Archive at Kew, the National Theatre Archive at Waterloo, and the team at Cliveden, including Angela and Erika, for making me so welcome. The online archive of *The Times*, dating back to 1785, is an underappreciated, indispensable resource.

I remain humbled not just that Morten Mørland agreed to provide the illustrations, but that he so brilliantly satirises the contemporary characters alongside the long-forgotten and the never-known. How a forty-something Norwegian can so perfectly capture Douglas Hurd, Pitt the Younger and Baby Gladstone is beyond me. It means this is now really an incredible collection of historical cartoons occasionally interrupted by my prose.

I was lucky to have great teachers, first at Huish Episcopi School, where Dave Roberts and Klim Deeley inspired a love of English and history respectively, something which continued at Richard Huish College with Jill Burton and Rob Johnson. My tutor and philosophy teacher Shelagh Evans was astonished that I might not go to university, but I hope that she is now reassured that things will pan out OK. To those I worked with at *Weekender*, *Taunton Times*, Press Association, *Western Morning News*, *Independent on Sunday* and *MailOnline*, I learnt something from all of you that I use every day.

I first met my wife, Alyson, at the *Taunton Times*. She found me irritating to start with. It is the risk that it might happen again which keeps me on my toes. Wherever my career has taken me, none of it compares to coming home to her afterwards. She tolerated all the things I neglected because I was 'writing a book'. I have a lot of catching up to do. I hope the mini-break to Barnard Castle goes some way to making amends. I'd also like to use this opportunity to remember Alyson's dear mum, Denise, who grew up in Lossiemouth, to where Ramsay MacDonald understandably retreated. In 2017 we all took the sleeper train to walk on Lossie's golden sands, and in her reminisces Denise was as happy as I'd ever seen her. We all miss her. Emily and Jessica are the daughters lesser parents dream of: kind, clever and, most important of all, wickedly funny. They make me laugh and make me proud every day. I've missed too many of their birthdays thanks to party conferences but hope I've made up for it in the other fifty weeks of the year.

I have been blessed with a vast, supportive family, of aunts, uncles and cousins. Since childhood my life has been peppered with people who questioned what I was doing. I listened instead to my incredible gran, Granny Spaxton, Gladys Speed, who is perhaps the greatest influence in my story. When others suggested I give up this nonsense and knuckle down to a proper job, she encouraged me to write that daft sketch show, apply for that job I was underqualified for, book that stand-up tour, and even have another performance of my TV show from inside the cardboard box in her front room. She indulged it all. I hope I've repaid a fraction of her belief.

Matt Chorley
Fleet, Hampshire
July 2023
matt@mattchorley.com

# Bibliography

Kieran Andrews and David Clegg, *Break-Up: How Alex Salmond and Nicola Sturgeon Went to War*, Biteback, 2021

Paddy Ashdown, *The Ashdown Diaries*, Penguin, 2001

Tony Blair, *A Journey*, Random House, 2010

Richard Bourne, *Lords of Fleet Street: The Harmsworth Dynasty*, Taylor & Francis, 2017

Gordon Brown, *My Life, Our Times*, The Bodley Head, 2017

Chris Bryant, *Parliament: The Biography*. Volume 2, Transworld, 2014

David Cameron, *For the Record*, William Collins, 2019

Rory Carroll, *Killing Thatcher*, HarperCollins, 2023

Peter Catterall, *The Macmillan Diaries*, Vol. II, Pan Macmillan, 2012

Michael Crick, *Sultan of Swing: The Life Of David Butler*, Biteback, 2018

Michael Cockerell, *Unmasking Our Leaders*, Biteback, 2021

Andrew Cook, *Cash for Honours: The Story Of Maundy Gregory*, The History Press, 2008

Francis Elliott and James Hanning, *Cameron: Practically A Conservative*, 4th Estate, 2012

Nigel Farage, *Flying Free*, Biteback, 2010

Andrew Gimson, *Gimson's Prime Ministers: Brief Lives from Walpole to Johnson*, Vintage, 2018

William Hague, *William Pitt the Younger: A Biography*, HarperCollins, 2004

David Laws, *Coalition*, Biteback, 2017

Andro Linklater, *Why Spencer Perceval Had To Die*, Bloomsbury, 2012

Adam Macqueen, *Private Eye: The 60 Yearbook*, Private Eye Productions, 2023

Adam, Macqueen, *Private Eye: The First 50 Years*, Private Eye Productions, 2011

John Major, *The Autobiography*, HarperCollins, 1999

David Marquand, *Ramsay MacDonald*, Metro Books, 1997

Patrick Marnham, *The Private Eye Story*, HarperCollins, 1982

Charles Moore, *Margaret Thatcher: The Authorised Biography*, Volume One: *Not For Turning*

Austen Morgan, *J. Ramsay MacDonald*, Manchester University Press, 1987

John Morley, *The Life of William Ewart Gladstone*, Cambridge University Press, 2011

Mark Pack, *Polling UnPacked*, Reaktion, 2022

Matthew Parris, *Chance Witness*, Penguin, 1997

William Pitt, *Correspondence of William Pitt, Earl of Chatham*. Volume 4, Cambridge University Press, 2013

John Preston, *A Very English Scandal*, Viking, 2016

Gabriel Pogrund and Patrick Maguire, *Left Out: The Inside Story of Labour Under Corbyn*, Vintage, 2020

Christopher Reindorp, *Never Shaken, Never Stirred: The Story of Ann Fleming and Laura, Duchess of Marlborough*, Biteback, 2023

Tim Ross and Tom McTague, *Betting The House*, Biteback, 2017

Tim Shipman, *All Out War*, HarperCollins, 2017

Margaret Thatcher, *The Downing Street Years*, HarperCollins, 1993

Nicklaus Thomas-Symonds, *Nye: The Political Life of Aneurin Bevan*, Bloomsbury, 2016

Harry Thompson, *Richard Ingrams: Lord of the Gnomes*, William Heinemann, 1994

D. R. Thorpe, *Selwyn Lloyd*, Vintage, 1989

# Index